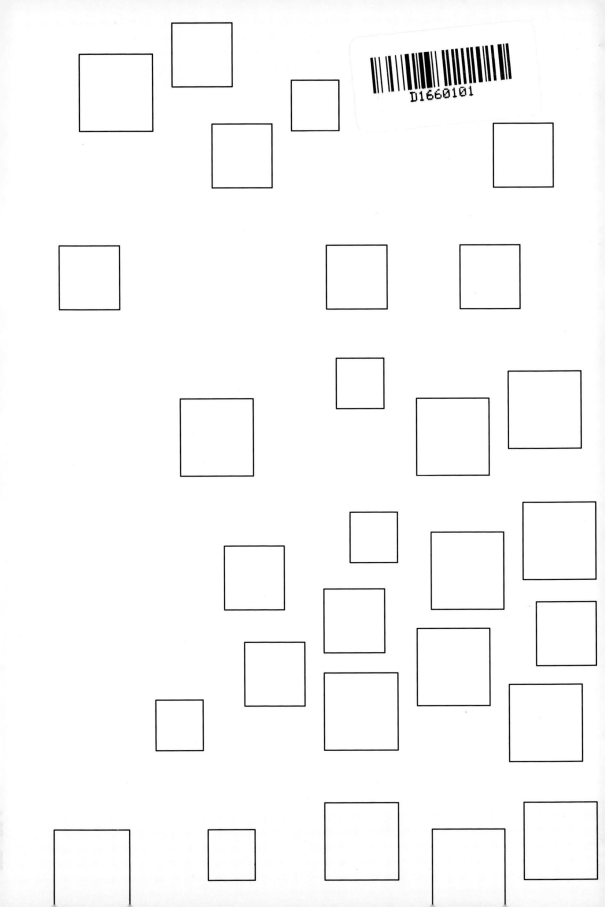

EDITED BY KRISTIN FEIREISS

WITH CONTRIBUTIONS BY
FLORIS ALKEMADE, NICOLE BERGANSKI,
RALPH BRUDER, KRISTIN FEIREISS,
KAZUYO SEJIMA + RYUE NISHIZAWA,
MATTHIAS SCHULER, TOM SIEVERTS,
DEYAN SUDJIC AND ROLAND WEISS

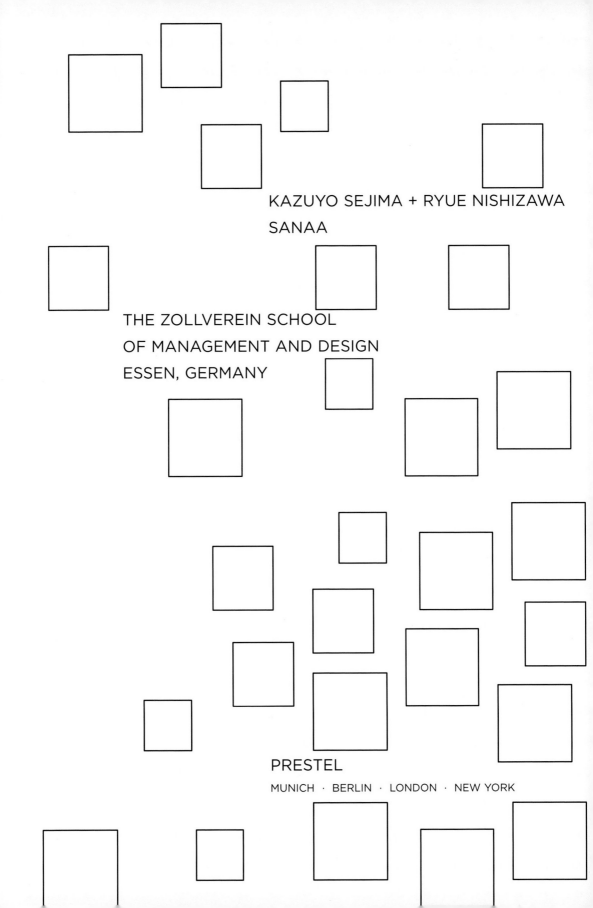

KAZUYO SEJIMA + RYUE NISHIZAWA
SANAA

THE ZOLLVEREIN SCHOOL
OF MANAGEMENT AND DESIGN
ESSEN, GERMANY

PRESTEL
MUNICH · BERLIN · LONDON · NEW YORK

CONTENTS

THE COMPETITION 7

PREFACE 8
KRISTIN FEIREISS

GENIUS LOCI ZOLLVEREIN 10
ROLAND WEISS

THE ZOLLVEREIN MASTERPLAN 16
FLORIS ALKEMADE / OMA

FROM COMPETITION TO REALISATION 22
THOMAS SIEVERTS

THE COMPETITION CONTRIBUTION 26
KAZUYO SEJIMA + RYUE NISHIZAWA / SANAA

THE ENERGY OF AN IMAGINARY SPACE 38
KRISTIN FEIREISS

REFLECTIONS 43

THE LIGHTNESS OF BEING 44
DEYAN SUDJIC

AN INTERVIEW WITH
KAZUYO SEJIMA AND RYUE NISHIZAWA 60
KRISTIN FEIREISS

THE DESIGN PROCESS   67

THE ZOLLVEREIN SCHOOL OF MANAGEMENT
AND DESIGN: USING INNOVATIVE DESIGN
SKILLS ON BUSINESS MODELS   68
RALPH BRUDER

THE BUILDING SITE   114

THE CHRONOLOGY OF THE DESIGN
AND BUILDING PROCESS   76
RALPH BRUDER

KAZUYO SEJIMA + RYUE NISHIZAWA / SANAA   124

BUILDING DATA   126

THE ZOLLVEREIN SCHOOL OF
MANAGEMENT AND DESIGN 2003 – 2006   90
KAZUYO SEJIMA + RYUE NISHIZAWA / SANAA

THE AUTHORS   127

COLLABORATION BETWEEN
ENERGY AND DESIGN   108
MATTHIAS SCHULER AND NICOLE BERGANSKI

THE COMPETITION

KRISTIN FEIREISS

PREFACE

"It's all about context and process," say Kazuyo Sejima and Ryue Nishizawa, the congenial partners who make up the Japanese architectural practice SANAA, and this could also be taken as a description of their central design strategy. It is precisely this approach that provides the background to the development of the Zollverein School of Management and Design in Essen. This strategy also determined the way in which the two-phase competition for the new building was set up. The first phase was anonymous, while the second was conducted by means of dialogue with the teams of architects selected to further develop their design concepts. SANAA emerged as the winners of this second phase. But this was by no means the end to the dialogue. On the contrary, it signalled the start of an intensive period of collaboration with representatives of the client and the user. The final design was gradually arrived at by means of countless personal discussions on site, as well as telephone conversations and e-mails across thousands of miles. The goal was to link content and design in such a way that the building by SANAA would be the formal expression of the concept behind the Zollverein School of Management and Design. Rarely has the form of a building been so indissolubly linked from the very start with the programmatic goals of the user. This unique combined effort to find a solution demanded rarely matched levels of intensity and consistency and should hopefully set an example for others.

For these reasons, the design and the building itself are not being looked at in isolation in this, the first book about the Zollverein School of Management and Design, published to coincide with the inauguration of the building. Instead, the focus is placed on the dialogue between form and content and on the process-based approach. The central issue is the openness and willingness on both sides to engage in discussion, to take part in constructive confrontations, and jointly to develop solutions that achieve a unity of form and content.

One thing can already be said with certainty: Essen, recently selected as the European Capital of Culture in 2010, can offer visitors from all over the world an architectural highlight in the form of the Zollverein School.

ROLAND WEISS

GENIUS LOCI ZOLLVEREIN

"... The function of a building – where it is uncompromisingly understood and shaped accordingly – leads to architecture, to a new architecture that has its own laws."

This statement might almost be from our own times, as it seems so appropriate to the new building for the Zollverein School of Management and Design. But in fact this sentence was written about eighty years ago and is taken from the manifesto *Über neue Formen der Architektur* (On New Forms in Architecture) by Friedrich Schupp and Martin Kremmer, the two architects of Zollverein Pit XII and the coking plant. With their clean lines, reduced forms and calculated symmetry Schupp and Kremmer created an uncompromising and highly impressive industrial architecture. The building was developed from the inside out, focussing closely on its function. Innovative materials and technologies were employed and the need to provide a striking symbol was also taken into account. In this sense Zollverein Pit XII could be seen as an early example of corporate design, which is among the reasons that, in 2001, the former colliery and coking plant were included in the UNESCO World Cultural Heritage list.

Today this complex is the best-known industrial landmark site in the Ruhr district. There is a rich diversity of activities on the site as a whole. The Zollverein has long since established itself as an attractive location for cultural events. Hundreds of thousands of tourists from throughout the world visit the site each year and, in 2010, when Essen becomes the European Capital of Culture, the Zollverein will play a central role both for Essen and the Ruhr district as a whole.

An impressive dynamism is developing in the area of design. Back in the 1990s the direction that was to be taken by the new Zollverein was indicated when the Design Zentrum Nordrhein Westfalen moved into Norman Foster's conversion of the former Pit XII boiler house. Today, the Zollverein provides 1,000 jobs and new ones are being created. Creativity plays an important role with interdisciplinary cooperation being a fundamental prerequisite for design-related 'added value'. In this field the Zollverein offers ideal conditions. The intellectual and physical network formed by the Zollverein School of Management and Design and the new designstadt Zollverein, the mix of theory and practice, the cooperation between design offices, engineers, architects and researchers, the proximity of recently set-up companies and established firms is what constitutes the attractiveness of the new Zollverein. An important impulse will come from the exhibition 'ENTRY2006 – Wie werden wir morgen leben?' (ENTRY2006 – How will we live tomorrow?), to run from 26 August to 3 December 2006, which will offer a view of the future of design. Centrally located in the recently opened, former coal washing plant, 300 objects from more than 20 countries will be displayed in five sections designed by well-known curators from the USA and Germany. There will be an accompanying programme of about 60 additional events. The Zollverein School of Management and Design, the impressive flagship of the new Zollverein, will also be used as a location.

The architects Kazuyo Sejima and Ryue Nishizawa from SANAA have succeeded in creating a most impressive building by unswervingly focussing on its function and engaging in the closest possible cooperation with the future users. The use of innovative building technology, in particular the 'active' thermal insulation in which warm water from the mine circulates in the external facades, allows the use of a spatial aesthetic that reflects the open and dynamic spirit of the Zollverein School in the areas of teaching, research and practice. This bright cube is the first new building to be erected on the Zollverein site since the completion of the coking plant in the 1950s. This makes the opening in June 2006 an historic date and allows us to view the building as a synonym for the new Zollverein.

ROLAND WEISS
MANAGING DIRECTOR,
ENTWICKLUNGSGESELLSCHAFT ZOLLVEREIN MBH
(ZOLLVEREIN DEVELOPMENT COMPANY LTD.)
ESSEN, MAY 2006

FLORIS ALKEMADE / OMA

THE ZOLLVEREIN MASTERPLAN

Despite its size of around 100 hectares the hermetic character of the Zollverein colliery means that it remains largely concealed from the outside world. Furthermore, the three large industrial complexes located on the site are now more or less isolated from each other so that their original close connection is hardly perceptible any longer.

When defining a new future for the Zollverein it was important that the complex should open up and that the original coherence be recreated. Interaction between new programmes can set a process in motion in which the strong identity of the Zollverein can function as the motor for future developments that, today, can only be envisaged to a limited extent. The masterplan therefore focuses on creating openness as well as defining the context. To strengthen the historical identity and context, the new building has been deliberately located on the periphery. At the same time the railway yard, with its marvellous patterns, has been transformed into a freely accessible area that makes the new complexes visible from within while simultaneously opening them up.

Where this public area meets the outside world large new entrances have been created that function like huge windows making the Zollverein visible and liberating it from its isolation. Each of these entrances is provided with an 'attractor': an expansive, open function that gives each of the new 'Zoll-houses' a face.

The Zollverein School, along with the newly planned Ruhr Museum and the visitors' centre in the old coal washing plant, is one of these three attractors. It is connected to the large public area and also to a second axis leading to one of the two business parks to be developed on the site. This creates an optimum connection with both the public and production programmes. The Zollverein School thus lies at the junction of production and consumption. Focusing on the design tasks of the future, it connects the worlds of economy and design and forms an attractive counterpart to the historical context of the area. It demonstrates that the Zollverein is not a dead monument and that, rather than coming to a standstill, its evolution is still in progress, using the same daring and revolutionary architecture as at the start of its history.

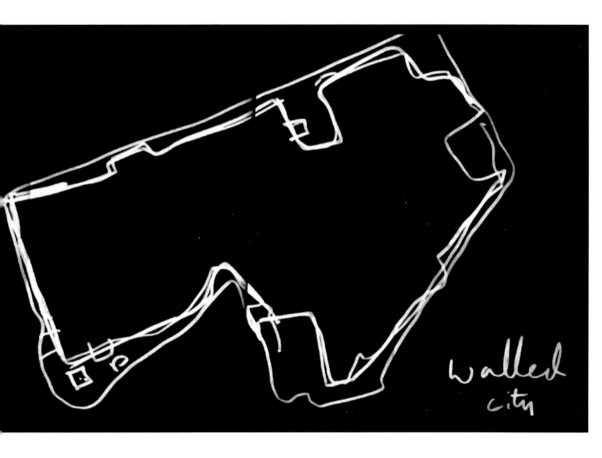

inner zone

attractors

business

green

infrastructure

railway tracks

time

FLORIS ALKEMADE / OMA   THE ZOLLVEREIN MASTERPLAN

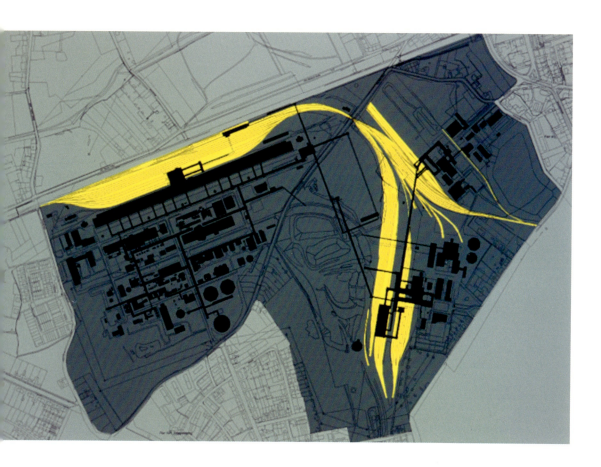

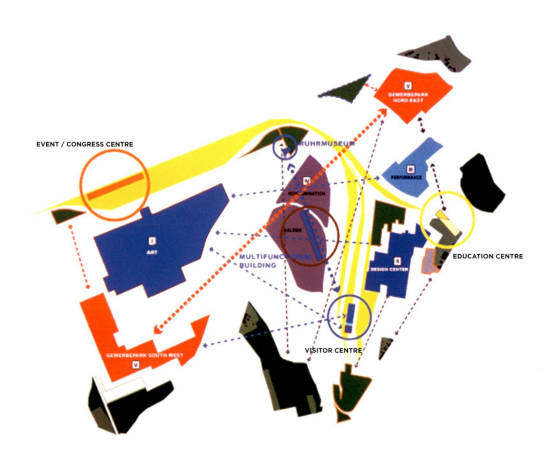

THOMAS SIEVERTS

FROM COMPETITION TO REALISATION

As a rule, not just in Germany but in all central European countries, architectural competitions are held for the design of public buildings. This is a sensible tradition, as it offers a number of alternatives and allows the best design to be selected and built. Experience has shown that competition entries rarely go so far beyond the conventional design concept as to unsettle the jury by offering new and daring ideas. In general juries find themselves on familiar ground where they can safely make their decisions.

However, there are also architecture competitions where the jury is confronted with new and unusual designs. In such cases the discussions can lead to an adventure with an uncertain outcome. Is the design, although original, burdened with the risk of disappearing under the pressure exerted by the practical business of construction planning or, even worse, is there a danger that a building could be built without being able to fulfil, on a permanent basis, the function promised? The history of competitions is full of original ideas that, after only a few years, are of no interest to anyone. In such cases opting for a conventional but more 'long-lasting' solution that had already been tried and tested would have been better.

Or are jurors dealing with the rare case of a new innovative concept that is suitable for long-term development, with which, in the best-case scenario, a new chapter of building history can be written? And can they rely on the author (who remains anonymous during the assessment process) to minimise the risks inherent in executing the building, while not detracting from the original concept?

Here I can recall two particularly striking examples of successful, daring decisions made by a jury that opened the way for the further development of building history: the decision in favour of Scharoun's design for the Philharmonie building in Berlin and the selection of Behnisch's design for the Munich Olympic Centre complex.

A further example, comparable in nature if not in size, is the competition for the Zollverein School of Management and Design. It rarely happens in the course of jury meetings during an architecture competition that a project initially viewed with scepticism, a design that is minimalist, difficult and laconic in character, can, as a result of qualities revealed when analysed several times, gradually work its way so clearly to the front of the competition entries that it is finally unanimously awarded first prize.

And it is rarer still that a jury's hopes for the further development of the conceptual idea are met in a way that even surpasses what was conceivable at the time the decision was made.

jury meeting at the zeche zollverein

The demands on this new building are considerable, as the Institution for Management und Design has to integrate itself into part of a World Cultural Heritage site, the Zollverein XII colliery designed by the architects Schupp and Kremmer. At the time the original colliery buildings were erected the architects succeeded in convincing the client that the various elements making up the works should not be placed under a single, large roof (which would have been the cheaper solution) but, instead, to erect a strictly geometric composition of cubes of brick, glass and steel that, with minimised, common, structural elements and through the use a rigorous, overall, geometric order were corseted together to produce an architectural work of art.

The content sought for this historically unique colliery complex in the context of the IBA Emscher Park consists – in broad terms – of creative facilities. With such uses this industrial *gesamtkunstwerk* moves beyond its significance as an important symbol of the industrial age to become, at one and the same time, a symbol of the new era of a 'society of knowledge'. Following this concept the new uses are not restricted to the historically important buildings. Instead, the entire colliery complex will be expanded into a ring by adding new areas, based upon a concept devised by Rem Koolhaas. The new design school will be erected in the surroundings of new cultural uses but with a direct relationship to the historic complex. The architects are the competition winners Kazuyo Sejima and Ryue Nishizawa with their Tokyo-based practice SANAA. The local contact architects are Heinrich Böll and Hans Krabel, who were earlier responsible for the conservation work on the historic complex.

The design of the Japanese architects group is as minimalist as the architecture of Schupp and Kremmer: a sharp-edged, bright cube measuring 35 × 35 × 34 m. The reduction helps the new design to relate to the formal idiom of the historic complex.

But this is where the similarities end. In contrast to the Cartesian clarity of the historic complex that was clearly influenced by Mies van der Rohe, the building by the Japanese architects is a kind of irritant; due to the lack of a clear separation into floors and the irregular fenestration, i.e. the lack of a familiar standard of comparison, it is impossible to read the height or the internal layout of the building.

The irregular swarm of dissimilar windows is – as Glenn D. Lowry, the Director of the Museum of Modern Art in New York, remarked on looking at the model, "like the impact of jazz on a classical composition." The doctrine of functionalism has also been abandoned, as no functions can be clearly identified from outside. This makes one all the more curious about the interior

which – in contrast to the exterior – develops a functional clarity from bottom to top.

All the essential characteristics of this architecture were recognisable at the competition design stage, but at that time it was not yet possible to assess whether they could in fact be carried out. During construction planning it has been possible to enhance these qualities even further – and, to a certain extent in a surprising way – because the designers did not have to struggle with current building regulations, which (for the perfectly valid reason of energy saving) stipulate highly insulated walls and windows (regulations that did not exist in the 1920s and most certainly not for industrial buildings).

These regulations, necessary in standard cases, would inevitably have greatly reduced the design's minimalist elegance, were it not for the application of high technical intelligence and the close cooperation of the client, architects and energy planner (Transsolar Stuttgart) to devise a completely different energy concept using the hot water in the pit (which in any case has to be pumped out) – a solution conceivable only at this old colliery location.

It is also the intelligent application of such a technical and historical source of energy that has allowed this remarkable building, with its physical form and inner creative life, to become an architectural landmark. It is a great historical transformation in which, following on from the era of coal and steel, knowledge and its creative application continue to form the basis of our civilisation.

The building now under construction in one sense stands in the tradition of classic modernism while also representing 'post-functional' architecture. Here a piece of 'absolute' architecture is being created, highly suitable for a design school where economy and creativity are to be integrated with each other, without the building exhausting its functional potential but remaining open for the unforeseeable.

ryue nishizawa and kazuyo sejima presenting their competition model

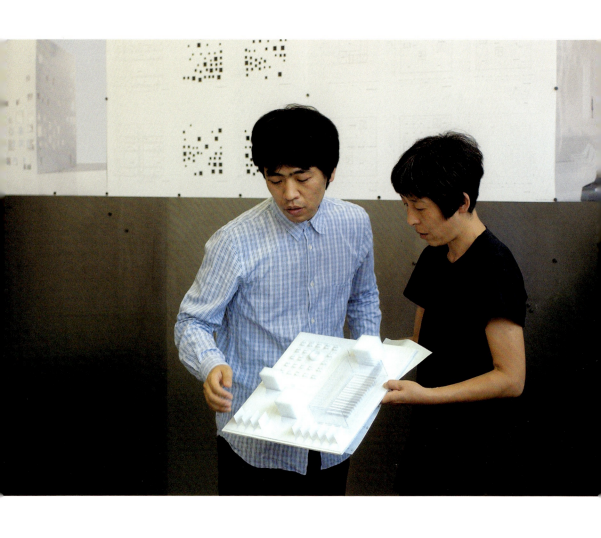

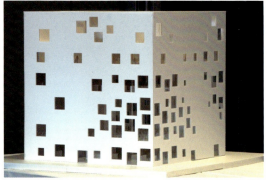

KAZUYO SEJIMA + RYUE NISHIZAWA / SANAA

THE COMPETITION CONTRIBUTION

On the border between an industrial site and suburbia we regard size as important. The volume creates an entrance to the whole area. We intend to charge the proximity between the units with vast differences in ambience. The Zollverein School of Management and Design is a large, new, sovereign element on the site. The Start Factory is a conversion of an existing structure. Student accomodation is exposed to an entirely different context, as we have divided the housing programme into small units throughout the Creative Village.

The external walls enclose the volume, yet the specific construction of these walls allows views of the surroundings and offers moderate natural illumination of the interiors. We see the façade as a filter to the surrounding landscape.

The section of the Zollverein School of Management and Design is a search for height where all floors can have lofty spaces, while allowing the structure as a whole to display clear differences in height.

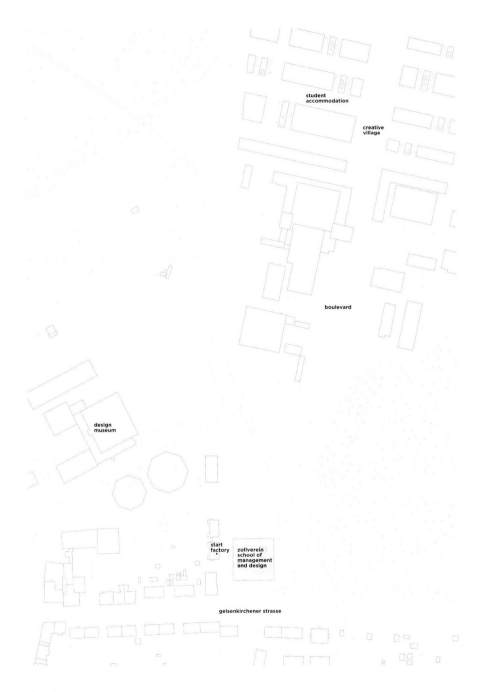

site plan

The building consists of stacked, open floor plans with varying ceiling heights which contribute to flexibility and diversity on all levels.

All spaces for public functions – the auditorium, the exhibition space and the cafeteria – are located on the ground floor.

Level 1 is the production floor with the design studio which boasts the greatest clear height to allow maximum flexibility.
Level 2 contains the library which is an introverted space in which the corners have been left free to be used as seminar rooms positioned against the façade.
On level 3 the workplaces are arranged along the façades and around a courtyard. This guarantees natural lighting. The roof has been conceived as a garden.

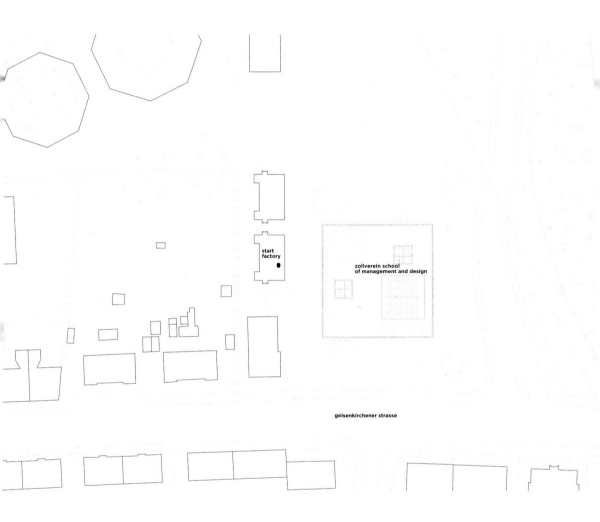

site plan, detail

KAZUYO SEJIMA + RYUE NISHIZAWA / SANAA   THE COMPETITION CONTRIBUTION

external view

internal view

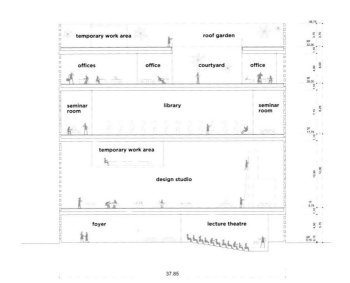

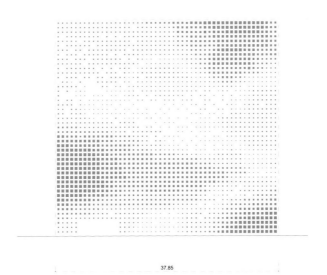

sections

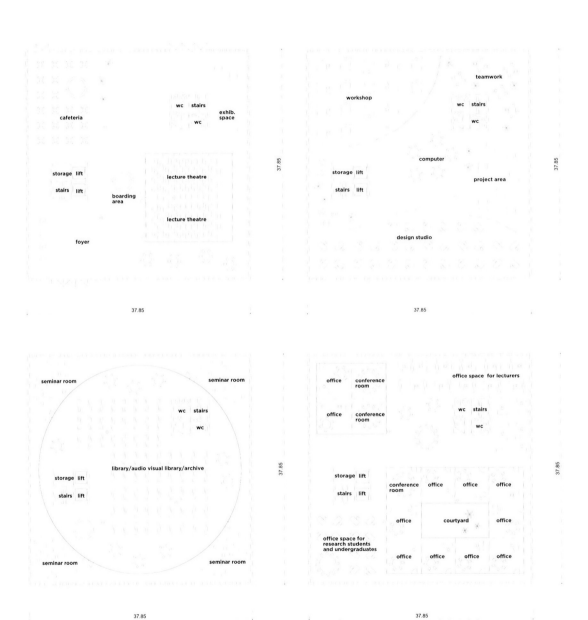

floor plans from top left to bottom right:
ground floor, first level, second level, third level

KAZUYO SEJIMA + RYUE NISHIZAWA / SANAA   THE COMPETITION CONTRIBUTION

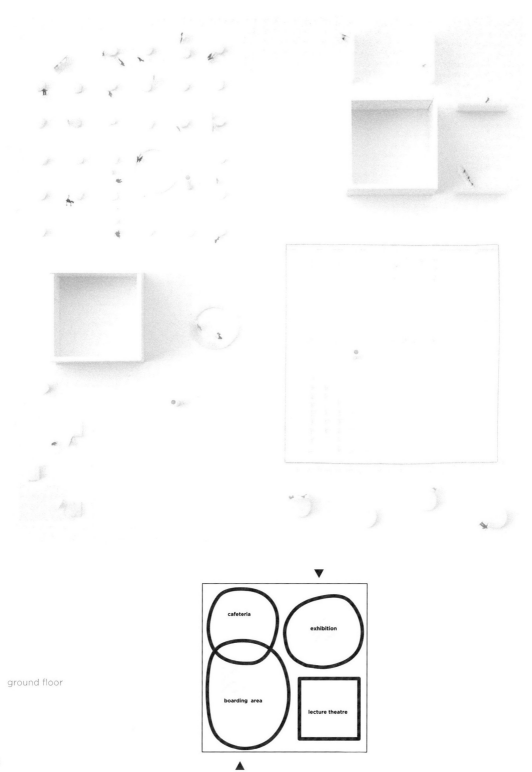

ground floor

level 1

KAZUYO SEJIMA + RYUE NISHIZAWA / SANAA   THE COMPETITION CONTRIBUTION

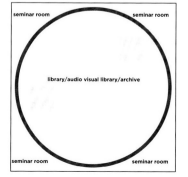

level 2

level 3

KRISTIN FEIREISS

THE ENERGY OF AN IMAGINARY SPACE

To write about architecture is in some way inherently contradictory. How can one make clear the 'additional' as Theodor W. Adorno calls it, the quality that goes beyond a building's functional use and suggests the artistic, the unmistakeable? Most attempts here fail from the start in the way they define the terms. And what can one do when one's own perception of the building cannot be used as a tool in the analysis and evaluation of an architectural design because the building has not yet been erected and one's senses, therefore, largely remain untouched by it?

The first cautious step to be taken before writing is reading, exploring the drawings, the floor plans, the façades and the sections, line-by-line. Sometimes one's eye is caught by numbers that say little to the uninitiated and which even those with the necessary skills have difficulty in translating into space. How do lines on paper create a space in the mind, long before that space is built – a space that defines itself in the field of tension between enveloping and demarcating? And how should one describe atmosphere as an element of an architecture that has not yet acquired a three-dimensional form?

It is not my aim to awaken sympathy for a profession that attempts to approach architecture using words. However, I do plea for an attempt to understand the difficulties of an undertaking that is obliged to make do with substitutes. As well as the study of plans and drawings the critic can also rely on a certain degree of specialist knowledge and experience that allows him or her to compare, assess and evaluate. Naturally, there are also the critic's powers of imagination that, given the lack of something concrete to look at, are indispensable. My experience as someone involved in writing is that one can only expose oneself to all these inadequacies when the examination of a design represents a challenge, even perhaps a provocation.

The prize-winning design for the Zollverein School on the site of the old Zollverein colliery in Essen, Germany, by the Tokyo-based, Japanese architecture practice, SANAA, is both a challenge, because the secrets of this design are not disclosed at first glance, and a provocation, because it departs from traditional ways of seeing.

On looking at the drawings initially there is nothing that the eye can fix on, nothing to capture the fleeting glance, no ornamental development of the façade, no meandering intertwining form, no high-tech image in gleaming steel, no colours with signal effects. Yet personally when studying the delicate competition entry drawings – that demand full concentration to understand them just as one must listen more attentively to someone who speaks in a soft voice – I could feel the energy of the imaginary space. The power of the cube is not dependent on fashionable trends or attempts to harmonise with the excellent industrial buildings nearby that date from a past era. A comment the architecture critic Wolfgang Hoffmann once made about SANAA's work also applies to this design: "The whole thing is not art, but art's primary form: space, pure space."

To achieve the highest possible quality when employing such apparent simplicity, sensitivity and professionalism are required in equal amounts. The young Japanese architecture practice has shown precisely these qualities in numerous projects it has already built.

I have been fortunate enough to experience the full effect of many of their buildings in Japan: the H-House in Tokyo in which all the storeys flow into each other, the Sashunkan Seiyaku housing development that, despite the predetermined size of the tiny living units, overcomes any possible feeling of restriction through transparency and a new living style, the platform studios for artists which connect the intimacy of living spaces with the generosity of the artist's studio and are placed under an accessible roof that is integrated into the landscape.

The search for the explanation of the SANAA phenomenon leads us to the native country of the architects Kazuyo Sejima and Ryue Nishizawa, that is to Japan – and to the father of Japanese modernism, Kazue Shinohara. Shinohara led Japanese architecture into a new era of poetic minimalism, marked by the symbiotic relationship between architecture and landscape, by the *engawa* – those intermediate zones in traditional Japanese architecture with *shoji*, paper sliding walls.

The achievements of Japanese modernism as reflected in the transformation of a tradition, the interrelation of inside and outside, the symbiosis of envelope and contents and the development of new kinds of building programmes have led to SANAA now occupying a central position in international, architectural discourse. In the words of Kazuyo Sejima's teacher, Toyo Ito, SANAA already have the status of an 'exception' and Iseku Hasegawa is convinced that the pair of architects even has 'the potential to start a social revolution'.

An important element of SANAA's architecture is what is rather inadequately described by the words 'building programme'. This was first introduced by Kazuyo Sejima and Ryue Nishizawa into the world of building in Japan where the concentration had previously been placed more on aesthetic questions. As in the design of the Zollverein School the architects have simplified and schematised this programme, thus bringing the functions of the building closer together, both spatially and in terms of content.

In the special context of the former colliery, the cube of the Zollverein School as suggested by SANAA not only unfolds its strength through its dimensions and materials, but also contributes to the inner harmony of the entire complex through a strong presence that is entirely free of any traces of preciousness.

The design of the massive concrete cube that is permeated by square windows in different sizes and arrangements – revealing an image, articulated in segments, of the activities inside – seeks to engage the users and the tall industrial buildings in its immediate surroundings in dialogue.

Both the design and the building programme share a common development process and the greatest possible degree of flexibility – aspects that are of central importance of the philosophy of the Zollverein School as developed by its founding director, Ralph Bruder. The intensive dialogue between all those involved in the design and in the content of the school will, in future, determine the spirit of this place.

kazuyo sejima with a model of the zollverein school

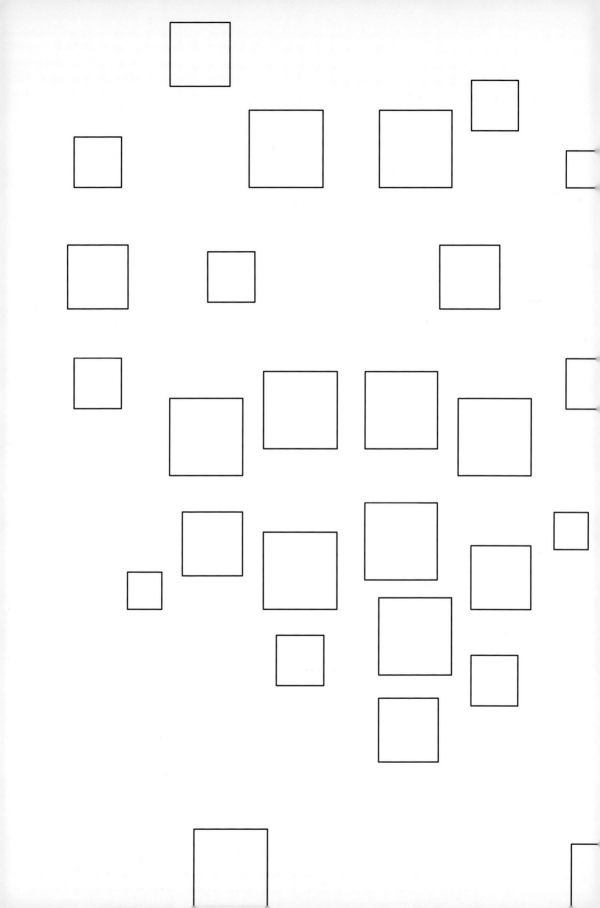

REFLECTIONS

DEYAN SUDJIC

THE LIGHTNESS OF BEING

A few years ago, I was a member of the jury for the European Union's Mies van der Rohe prize for contemporary architecture. Unlike too many of such awards, the process for awarding the Mies prize for the most distinguished building of the year in Europe makes considerable demands on jury members' time. After an initial paper exploration of nominated projects, there is a commitment to go and visit all the short-listed buildings rather than work on the basis of photographs and drawings. Which is how I, as the London based editor of the Italian magazine Domus, came to spend a week criss-crossing Europe, from Barcelona to Amsterdam with a group that included the English architect David Chipperfield, Aaron Betsky, the American critic who at that time was the director of the Netherlands Architecture Museum, Matthias Sauerbruch from Berlin and, as it happened, Kazuyo Sejima herself.

In a series of debates and conversations that began in the basement of Richard Meier's museum of modern art in Barcelona, and later moved to the 18th-century splendour of the French Institute of Architecture in Paris, Sejima was a quietly forceful presence, expressing a lucid clarity in her views of architecture. She argued for simplicity and straightforwardness, rather than artifice and formalism. It made her sound a little like one of those modernists from the 1930s who looked for a sense of moral mission in architecture that was 'honest'.

An award scheme is just one small aspect of the many and complex ways that an architectural climate of opinion is formed. But the decision making process was an intriguing insight into the mechanisms through which intellectual debate is pursued. It was an experience which served to highlight the way in which ideas can ricochet back and forth between continents, turning architecture into a borderless, placeless pursuit apparently existing in a vacuum in which the only points of reference are internal.

How many people actually get to experience new architecture in the way in which those jury members did; moving from city to city to spend an hour touring a building as if they were looking at art works on gallery walls, and then moving quickly on to the next in the series? Perhaps none, except for the delegations of museum trustees who customarily embark on a similar odyssey before selecting an architect for a new extension and who, as a result, find themselves developing a similar value system. Architecture as architecture is never experienced in this way. It is the interaction with place and people over long periods of time that really give it meaning.

It may be an isolated aberration, but for those who do experience architecture in the way of the Mies jury, it is a powerful incubator for the rapid transmission, or even cross infection of architectural attitudes. It creates a new way of perceiving architecture, as a kind of hermetic, self-contained culture, insulated from everything but the language of architects. It is only against such a background that one could explain hearing the suggestion that was voiced in the jury room, as we did, that to select Zaha Hadid for the prize, which she duly collected for designing a tram terminus in Strasbourg, was to be making a 'safe' choice. Hadid might be 'safe' in the virtual world of architectural prizes, but in the real world she is anything but. In the same way, it is worth remembering that Sejima is anything but a conventional practitioner as an architect. And yet, together with Ryue Nishizawa as SANAA, she has become one of the names that keeps materialising around the world, a winner of the Venice Golden Lion, short-listed for major competitions, and now beginning to build on an increasing scale in Europe and America as well as in Japan.

Moving across Europe at the Mies jury's pace is a chance to see the similarities and the differences between one architect and another, but in a way that inevitably divorces them from their context. And it has a tendency to encourage the creation of a kind of architecture aimed very specifically at that audience of critics and trustees and jurors who formulate and disseminate architectural reputations, and who direct new commissions accordingly. This self referential critical climate is a prerequisite for the current situation in which architectural careers have become borderless. They are measured now, not by the careful steps of commission following commission in a graded national progression from a house for a relative to a small gallery, to a museum based on the connections and generational shifts of a national culture, but on a giddying zigzag around the world. Architects can now find themselves projected from obscurity at home to celebrity abroad in a single leap. If anything, it is a pattern that reflects the careers of artists, measured out by their invitations to make an installation at every biennale from Kassel to São Paolo, rather than that of architects. It creates a kind of hothouse in which architectural ideas too fragile for the outside world can be nurtured until they are ready for wider exposure. Kazuyo Sejima, now working with Ryue Nishizawa as part of SANAA, is undoubtedly the product in part of this phenomenon.

But while it is clearly the case that there has never been a moment when quite so many high-profile buildings have been designed by so few architects, it is too simple a reading of the situation to see in this the reduction of architecture into some kind of single globalised norm. There is certainly a universal architectural conversation, like the one conducted by the Mies van der Rohe jury, that does take place in Basel and London, as well as Tokyo and Los Angeles. But emerging architectural voices, of which the SANAA studio is among the most distinctive, retain their individual qualities and a rootedness in time and place, no matter where they work. And there is a lot about SANAA that is specifically the product of their Japanese roots. Equally, SANAA's exceptionally sophisticated architecture has absorbed some of the currents that are flowing around the jury rooms and the prize-giving panels. They have explored the idea of blending walls with floors and have made a virtue of cheap, artificial materials.

It's true that SANAA leaves traces of their work in all kinds of unexpected places in a way that reflects the globalised architectural culture in which they operate. In the garden of Luis Barragan's house in Mexico City you could find a little knot of their chrome-plated steel chairs. SANAA was selected by the mayor of Salerno to take part in the transformation of the city. But in the way of things in Italy, there has been little progress in realising its competition winning scheme for re-vitalising the public spaces of Salerno's old town. And SANAA's name was part of Prada's plans for entrusting its identity to a group of high visibility architects. All of these projects are the result of its role in the global architectural conversation. But in the end, SANAA's architecture is the product of the special circumstances of contemporary Japan, where the outward forms of modernity have their own meanings, and which has arrived at its current state through a sequence of events that is all its own. SANAA's work overseas is now more extensive than it is in Japan, and Sejima and Nishizawa are becoming perhaps the first Japanese architects to have built their reputation by working primarily overseas.

Sejima was born in 1956, and grew up in a Japan that was fast joining the western world as a modern industrial power. Nishizawa is a child of the 1960s. Sejima was eight years old when Kenzo Tange's Olympic swimming pool in Tokyo set the seal on Japan's post war reconstruction, and its adoption of the language of modernism as an expression of national identity. Arata Isozaki had already established the basis of an alternative version of Japanese architecture before she became a student. After graduating, she spent several formative years in the early 1980s, working in the studio of Toyo Ito. It was Ito that represented the most considerable force in forging a new version of contemporary architecture in Japan. He succeeded the heroic form-givers of the Tange generation who had been heavily influenced by Le Corbusier, and produced a very different vision of architecture. And its not hard to find echoes of Ito's interest in lightweight ephemeral structures in her own work. Sejima admired Ito's architecture as a student, and remained close to him after she established her own office. This was the period in which Tokyo was in the throes of the bubble economy, and Ito worked on a number of projects that were only made explicable by a city in

the revitalization of the old quarter of salerno, italy

which an explosive inflation of land prices encouraged developers to keep valuable plots of land empty while they waited to cash in on price rises. In these circumstances it made sense to design temporary structures that could make use of these plots in the short term. Ito designed lightweight ephemeral structures for use as exhibition galleries and bars, knowing fully well that they would have an abbreviated life span, but without compromising on their material quality or technological sophistication.

It's a context in which self-conscious form-making would have seemed ridiculous. How can a building assume the weight of permanence when it has already been programmed to self destruct with a built in sell-by date? Ito in a way was realising the dreams of Archigram, of instant fix, responsive architecture, and so by implication is SANAA. And in reflecting this, there is a certain subversive edge to be found in their sensibility, one which has survived the studio's exposure to the fashion world and its work for Dior and Prada.

The Japanese architect Jun Aoki has usefully suggested that "the reason that Sejima is not an architect in the classical sense is that she creates, but at the same time tries to erase all traces of herself from what she creates." It suggests an attempt to expunge the egotism of the architect which has tended to overshadow architecture and has produced a string of signature buildings that have threatened to turn architecture into a species of branding. Instead she works with the diagrams imposed by programme, budget and zoning as the point of departure for her buildings.

What SANAA adds to what might be seen as a functionalist mix is its vision of a building as a seamless totality, rather than a collection of discrete entities. Talking of Platform 1, Sejima's earliest independent commission, a private house in a rural setting, she describes how she wanted to interrupt the sort of planning which presumes the discontinuity of people's movement. And it is not just the delicate floating quality of her architecture that is its most distinctive characteristic. What really marks her out is the rigour with which she interrogates the plan.

SANAA's modest studio in Tokyo is in the warehouse district, surrounded by taxi garages, and is accommodated in a cheerfully ramshackle industrial space that suggests an anything but corporate approach to architecture.

Ito himself only really started to build on a substantial scale after the end of the 20th century. Sejima was as slow to secure larger commissions when she established her own office, initially under her own name as Ito had been. There was a string of individual houses, built to the tightest of budgets, and a number of

dior omotesando, 2003

prada beauty prototype, 2000

Pachinko parlours: the gaming establishments that are a universal feature of the Japanese landscape. After a period running a studio on her own, she began to work as SANAA when she established her partnership with Nishizawa in 1995, the younger architect who had previously worked in her office.

Ito remained an influence after Sejima left his office. She was one of several designers he asked to work on aspects of the interior of the Mediatheque in Sendai, and she acknowledges his influence on the planning of the Gifu apartment block. This was her first work to attract attention outside Japan. There and in even more restricted works such as the tiny house SANAA built in Tokyo, they used sheer ingenuity to put a great deal into the most confined of spaces.

SANAA's path has been a reflection perhaps of the role of the political connections on which Japanese architectural careers depend, with one generation creating opportunities for the next only sparingly. And in this regard Arata Isozaki is a key figure, nominating Sejima (along with three other female architects) to work on the Gifu project, and also commissioning her to work on the Japanese pavilion for the Venice architecture biennale in 2000.

It is only now, as she approaches fifty that Sejima is finally moving beyond a domestic scale in her work.

After SANAA's white glass building for Dior on Tokyo's Omotesando fashion strip, close incidentally to Toyo Ito's similar programme for a fashion building for Tod's, SANAA has moved quickly. Their role at Dior was to provide a beautiful container for the various elements of the Dior range, handing over the interiors to the keepers of the Dior brand. The building is an eight-storey-high tower, wrapped in two translucent skins, the outer is glass, the inner one of Perspex, tattooed with a pattern of white stripes. In contrast, the Kanazawa museum for contemporary art allowed SANAA to work in the way they prefer, to start with the programme, and to base the design of the interior on it, and from that to create an exterior.

They have moved to a new scale and to a new range of activity. In the next two years SANAA will be opening a substantial addition to the Toledo Museum in Ohio, to house its collection of glass artefacts, in a free-standing glass pavilion, and a theatre in Almere, the Dutch new town masterplanned by Rem Koolhaas. The New Museum in New York got underway at the end of 2005. SANAA is working on an office building for Novartis in Basle. Taken together, they amount to an impressive argument for a new kind of approach to architecture.

SANAA stands against the massive, and the rhetorical, in architecture, and in favour of the delicate and light-

21st-century museum of contemporary art,
kanazawa, japan 2004

DEYAN SUDJIC THE LIGHTNESS OF BEING

21st-century museum of contemporary art,
kanazawa, japan 2004

weight. These are perhaps words that might be equated with femininity, a problematic subject to introduce into an architectural conversation, although given the strand of sweetness in Sejima's work, demonstrated by a recurring use of decorative daisy patterns, perhaps not entirely unjustified. But they are hardly adequate to describe what Sejima and Nishizawa are trying to do. They have an apparent aversion to mass and texture. There are times when their work appears to be the product of a sensibility that is closer to tatami than to Charles Eames. Though of course, Eames himself was fascinated by Japanese delicacy.

SANAA's approach amounts to an attempt at filtering architecture of all its excess baggage, by reducing building to a distilled essence, one that has nothing to do with chilly Puritanism. Drained of colour and gratuitous incident, theirs is an architecture from which iconography and narrative have been expunged, and replaced by a celebration of light and transparency. It is an architecture in which they claim to put the user and their needs at the heart of the design process.

"For the time being the method we are using is premised on the extremely modern idea of making the content of the building the human actions that take place within and create the architectural form," she describes it. For SANAA, it's important to treat every design as a new departure.

"Each project has its own method of adjustment, the process in itself constitutes a creative act." Her words make her sound a little like a born-again functionalist. And it is underscored by her belief that "our approach is to design from the inside out, the exterior expresses the interior, which is first the response to the clients programme."

But they also look in patterns of movement at both the intimate scale of the interior, as well as on the urban one. SANAA devised the Almere theatre as an urban block. The New Museum in New York responds to the scale of the context even if its iridescent metal skin makes it feel as if it is an object descended from another universe. SANAA suggests that "a museum for contemporary art should be neutral in the character of its gallery space in order to create the widest palette for the art. It must be possible to think about a new sort of flexibility to that of the past."

Their most significant tool is scale and planning: "We tried to play with dimensions. The New Museum is very open and not afraid to take a stand, and in constant dialogue with different forces in society. The client and we, as architects, wanted to make a building that expresses this openness, this independence, and this fascination with the world we live in. So SANAA designed a straightforward building. All of our designs are programme driven, we have a strong desire to relate programmes to one another in an open and non directional way. We try to create different experiences for the visitor, and generate a freedom to explore."

This is a mood that informs SANAA's working methods as well as their finished designs. Their exquisite models demonstrate the eye of a designer who revels in artificiality, and the denial of mass. And SANAA's elegant drawings, strongly graphic but with great economy of means suggest a refinement of a singular strand in architectural modernity. SANAA's drafting technique represents their projects in a highly suggestive way, as do the models. Sejima and Nishizawa present their work as if it were entirely artless, brutally diagrammatic almost. Again it is an attitude that seems to reflect some of the interest that the high-tech movement had in the found object. But it is a sharp counterpoint to the energy and effort that SANAA pours into working with the proportions and scale of the buildings they design, and the care with which they approach the visual qualities of the skins with which they clad their buildings.

"We play with light and dimensions more than anything," SANAA has said.

There is an underlying oscillation in all the work, between structure and skin, between solid and void, transparent and translucent. "We have always been attracted by this ambivalence between something and nothing, by this floating identity of materials and space."

This may be a fresh incarnation of what was once called 'high tech', enriched with a more poetic sensibility and stripped of its fetishistic obsession with perforated metal and exposed structures. It is the root of a dissonance between the ephemerality of the building, where walls and windows dissolve, and where materials reveal their artificiality, even banality.

SANAA clearly has an allergy to monumentalism, to buildings that are based on the idea of creating form. Nor are their designs based in a search for the jewellery like precision of detail. In a way that is unusual in the present architectural climate, SANAA is fascinated by the way that they can use the organisation of planning to make spaces work and inject their buildings with radical possibilities.

SANAA is keen to keep its options open. They attempt to work without a signature, but there is no question that their work is readily identifiable. There is the issue of glass, which is part of their preferred palette. "I'm not so much interested in glass as a material. An important factor for my work is how the construction of a building is realised, the way the pieces are put together, rather than making the structure visible.

the toledo museum of art glass pavilion, toledo, ohio, usa

stadstheater almere 'de kunstlinie', almere, the netherlands

novartis campus wsj-158 office building, basle, switzerland

I guess it's the structure itself that I always want to be as clear as possible. Glass can break, but it is also a very durable material. Even after years glass always makes a building look newer than it actually is. It shows only faint signs of ageing. While the atmosphere of a brick building matures with time and metal panels look down-at-heel the older they get, glass is a material that almost doesn't change. Maybe that is actually a negative characteristic."

For SANAA, glass is not to be read in the most obvious way. "We think of transparency in conceptual rather than literal terms. In general we believe buildings should be open and communicative, not bastions. For the New Museum we tried to design a transparent building in the sense that we are not hiding what is happening behind the surface of the structure. The skin creates one kind of experience, but the structure's exterior also reveals the building's purpose. By shifting the programmatic boxes, we are allowing in daylight. We are creating views into and out of the interior and we are enjoying relationships with the building's surroundings. This strategy brings a certain lightness in character."

But the glass is also a sign of their interest in creating a recessive, permissive architecture, rather than an aggressive, formal language. "We do not believe that the architecture of a museum should dictate its use."

"The museum buildings we admire are those that use daylight as an architectural element." Sejima cites the courtyard of Renzo Piano's de Menil museum in Houston, the Pompidou in Paris and the Louisiana museum in Denmark as particular inspirations.

Speaking of the New Museum, and its collision with Manhattan's grid, she defines the biggest challenge facing them now as finding a way to achieve an ambitious programme without making a massive building. "How do you bring lightness to a heavy context without being blown away?" It's a question that could be said to encapsulate the nature of this stage of SANAA's output. On the basis of their work to date, its clear that they have already indicated that they have the answer.

In the midst of the heavy world of industry and mining, with its abandoned shafts and winding gear, the pit baths and the changing rooms that once seemed to represent enlightenment, SANAA's new school of management and design is a literal and symbolic signal of change and regeneration. It stands apart from the monumental industrial ruins of the Zollverein's glory days, but is not part of the local urban context either. It differentiates itself by its deference and lack of self assertion, rather than through any kind of aggression or bombast. But while it is detached from its surroundings, it does not deny, or ignore them. The past here is weighed down with negative associations. The future,

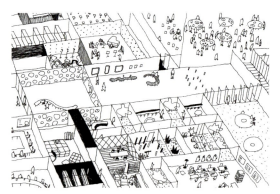

DEYAN SUDJIC THE LIGHTNESS OF BEING

new museum of contemporary art, new york, usa

as represented by the school, is presented as weightless and evidently light enough to shake off gravity altogether. It is concerned with the world of the mind, rather than the physicality of heavy labour, and its architecture eschews any trace of mass. It's a white cube, but a cube that is pierced both in scale with its fine mesh cladding and, on a broader level, with the syncopated rhythm of its window openings that conceal as much as they reveal about the nature of the building and its interior, with its subtle shifts in changes of level. It's a skin that will serve not to filter out the past, for the students who will use the school's studios and its auditoria, but will recontextualise it, framing it and making it part of a pattern.

SANAA have the impressive capacity of producing a floor plan that, at first sight, appears to be a functional diagram and then emerges as a carefully worked out, architectural response to the essence of the brief. The building avoids both hierarchical and bureaucratic planning. This is neither a blandly uniform interior, nor one of melodramatic ostentation. It attempts to be the background for a new kind of education, for a subject that is itself rapidly changing. It avoids corridors, and circulation. It offers a range of spaces of different character, related to each other through varying degrees of transparency, that is one of the defining characteristics of SANAA's work, and their fascination with inscribing circles in squares. In Germany of all places, a design school is the most charged of architectural commissions. From Dessau to Weimar architecture has been used to make pedagogical and philosophical statements about the nature of design education. Those schools themselves became emblematic of what they taught. And in their own way, SANAA's partners have not flinched from the challenge of doing the same.

model of the zollverein school

KRISTIN FEIREISS

AN INTERVIEW WITH
KAZUYO SEJIMA AND RYUE NISHIZAWA

K. F. You are working on your first construction project in Germany and, as such, are introducing yourselves at one of Europe's most important industrial monuments with an exiting project of powerful impact. With your project at the Zeche Zollverein in Essen – as well as at the Novartis Campus in Basle – you are building in an industrial context. How does your architecture react to the challenges of an urban context on a peripheral site?

K. S. + R. N. The situation in Essen is truly remarkable. In the case of the Zeche Zollverein we were really excited when we visited the site for the first time. We immediately thought about how we could create a positive and open relationship with such remarkable surroundings. The site is very interesting for us because it is so very different from our projects in Japan. The Zollverein site is dynamic and the scale overwhelming, yet the building structures in themselves are delicate. Our aim was to design a new building which refers to the scale of the former coalmine buildings. Normally we start to think about the scale of our buildings from the point of view of the programme and the activities that happens there, but in our project for the Zeche Zollverein we preferred to start thinking a bit more about the situation of the site and its surroundings. From the very beginning we decided to propose a big volume. In another setting a building with the same programme as the Zollverein School would have to be much smaller.

K. F. What was the reason for you to choose concrete as a building material? Obviously this material is totally different from that of the existing historical buildings of the Zeche Zollverein which are made out of steel cased in brick.

K. S. + R. N. At the beginning we actually thought about using brick, but we don't have enough experience using this material and, on the other hand, we didn't want to use a steel structure covered in glass. It would become too transparent and we didn't want our design to evolve in that direction. Our concept was to create a more massive, more powerful building by using concrete. Steel structures are also very expensive in Germany.

K. F. With your decision to create a big cube, a monolithic building in relation to the surroundings, you have set a powerful signal.

K. S. + R. N. The big volume of our building was necessary not only as a reaction to the site but also so that a dialogue with the remarkable historic buildings could be created. We have tried to make one volume which shows

ryue nishizawa and kazuyo sejima

continuity with the other big buildings, and we have kept a wide open space around our building as a reference to the site.

K. F. You decided on a strong concrete building but at the same time you have developed a kind of transparency. How did you manage to create this impression?

K. S. + R. N. It sounds like a paradox, but it was our intention to make the concrete transparent by adding a number of openings, but this transparency is totally different from the transparency achieved using glass. For us the thickness of the concrete wall, or rather the thinness, is as important as the penetration of windows to achieve a feeling of transparency.

K. F. The windows are a very significant element of the design. What was the concept behind these?

K. S. + R. N. Massiveness and light – both were important qualities for us to achieve continuity on the site. The windows, or rather the holes or openings are a strong element in achieving this aim. We always checked the different elevations with the client and the users, because the windows naturally have an impact on the interior as well as the exterior expression. Towards Gelsenkirchner Strasse or from the Zollverein site itself we wanted to make the envelope very open and transparent, and also from the opposite corner the interior can open up and show a view of the coalmine. Other parts of the interior, for example where those inside are working at the computer, we have proposed just a few windows purely related to the functional aspects of the use of the interior.

K. F. How was it possible to reduce the thickness of the concrete wall to underline the transparent impression of the building?

K. S. + R. N. The idea of using pit water for an active insulation of the building offered the possibility of having a thin concrete façade. Due to this technical concept, the normally required three layers of a concrete exterior wall – a 25 cm, load-bearing concrete wall, an insulation layer, and an exposed concrete layer – could be combined into a single-layer concrete wall. Integrated pipes provide thermal insulation for the entire building. The required dimension of the load-bearing concrete wall, including space for the pipes, is at 30 cm considerably less than to the 50 cm

for a normal 3-layered wall. The concept is based on water being pumped from the mineshafts 1,000 metres below ground level. The coalmine water is warm but contaminated, and is run through a heat exchanger connected to a separate system of pipes, providing active insulation for the Zollverein School.

K.F. By developing this principle you are also making a conceptual contribution to the site and the former use of the Zeche Zollverein. Have you ever developed such a concept before?

K.S. + R.N. This is the first time that we have designed a building like this. There was an opportunity to use the energy of the site and we found that very interesting.

K.F. Like many of your buildings in recent years, such as museums, theatres or educational facilities, the Zollverein School is a public building. We are interested in how you define the demand of buildings that serve a public function. What are the important criteria for the internal organisation and the use of a public building for you?

K.S. + R.N. In general, we are very interested in public buildings, in creating public space. Our intention or our understanding of public space, is seeing it as a kind of park. A park offers something for everybody and can absorb different generations, people of different social backgrounds, individuals or groups. We want to create this kind of public space inside buildings. In a museum visitors want to see the objects on display, but they also need a place to rest, to eat or to meet people, or simply to be alone. We don't like regulations and in general we allow visitors as much freedom as possible. But at the same time, a public building needs some regulations and a framework. We try to find a satisfactory balance.

K.F. You talked about public buildings from the aspect of their internal organisation. Do you think that public buildings should give out a signal?

K.S. + R.N. The programme of a public building has some special features from the outset. There may be, for example, one or two theatres in a city. That means you have to be aware of the importance of the building through its architecture. For this reason public buildings often have a strong impact to their surroundings due to their scale. We prefer to interpret public buildings, mainly cultural buildings, like mountains in a landscape. That means

a public building should never lose the natural relation to its surroundings. For us it is more important that people who visit our public buildings have a good experience and like to come back. This is much more important to us than impressing them with bombastic gestures.

K.F. Talking about your design process, do you develop your design strategy according to a particular commission and context of a project, or do you have basic criteria for a fundamental design strategy?

K.S. + R.N. We always start from making a volume based on the arrangement of the programme. Our design strategy in general is to relate the volume to the context. We always start from this point. Sometimes when the programme is very complex, we try to find out what the most interesting issue is. We always set priorities: it is an intensive process within our team to find the most important issues in each project.

K.F. Do you develop your design concept using models?

K.S. + R.N. It is important for us to design with models, but we also make sketches, drawings and plans in order to approach a problem using different kinds of representation and methods of thinking. But it is true, models are crucial for our process. More recently we have also been making photomontages, using photos of the site and its surroundings and combining them with model photos. Our design process begins literally from two different views, from two directions. One is to get a strong idea and feeling for the site, from a certain distance if you like; the other approach is to concentrate on the programme itself. In our design process we always focus on the programme and the volume and – very importantly – the structure. We believe structure has a major influence on the atmosphere of a building, both inside and out. If we have to choose, we spend more money on the structural elements and less on the material. After combining these three issues – programme, volume and structure – we decide how to move ahead and gradually we start making detailed drawings. Decisions on such issues as finishing materials and the development of the façade, for example, come later.

K.F. The Kunstlinie Theatre and Cultural Centre in Almere in the Netherlands, realised not so long ago, was your first project in Europe, and many more have followed in the past few years. Is there a difference between working in Japan and working in Europe and what is your experience of building in Europe?

the sanaa office in tokyo

KRISTIN FEIREISS AN INTERVIEW WITH KAZUYO SEJIMA AND RYUE NISHIZAWA

K.S. + R.N. We have been working on projects in Europe for seven years but none of our buildings have been finished yet. The Zollverein School will be the first, and I feel it is difficult to talk about experience before this is finished. But our general impression is that, in Europe, people try to think more about the spatial possibilities available and are more experimental. In Japan clients prefer to develop similar buildings to the existing ones, as ordinary as possible. Japanese developers don't like experiments.

K.F. How do you regard your work in Germany and in Europe in general and to what extent have you introduced your cultural Japanese background into your European projects?

K.S. + R.N. We never refer to anything from Japanese traditional buildings. We don't have a different attitude to our projects in Japan or in Europe. It is all about the context. That is the decisive factor. We do not transform Japanese elements into our own architectural language. We might be inspired by history or tradition, but this could come from any country or culture.

K.F. Seeing and analysing your œuvre it is obvious that your don't like big gestures. Your projects, even when some of them have large volumes, are very minimalistic.

K.S. + R.N. That's true. We are minimalists. But we distinguish between two directions in the minimalist movement. We don't want to make formally minimal architecture which might be very strict and rigid. In other words, we try to make our buildings very simple and straightforward, but the most important thing for us is that people enjoy the spaces we create.

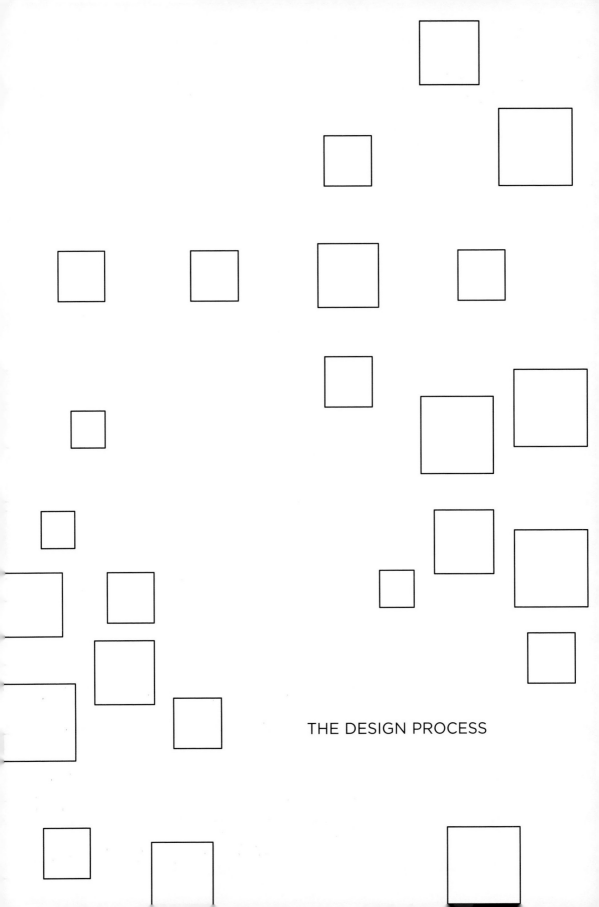

THE DESIGN PROCESS

RALPH BRUDER

THE ZOLLVEREIN SCHOOL OF MANAGEMENT AND DESIGN: USING INNOVATIVE DESIGN SKILLS ON BUSINESS MODELS

The economic significance of design is undisputed. In a complex environment characterised by a wide diversity of products, which are often difficult to tell apart, and a plethora of communication opportunities, design allows us to draw the valuable attention of potential customers to specific products. Today, design is already the decisive economic factor in several branches of industry, including the automotive and consumer goods industries.

The application of design is not limited to material goods alone – whether produced industrially or presented in virtual form. It is also increasingly employed in the creation of products in the service sector.

Today, businesses, regions and even countries are all faced with the problems of positioning themselves and creating an identity for themselves in a global environment. This is why they are increasingly turning to design for assistance. With all the focus on short-term issues, the stock exchanges and balance sheets, one thing has been somewhat forgotten in recent times: attitude and identity have always been the way to a company's success. These are the things that make a company stand out on the market. The appearance of products is a consequence of this. The shaping of identity is, therefore, a competitive strategy for the future. The linking of culture and business is the quintessential strength of design.

Studies conducted by the British Design Council show that companies improve both their productivity and their competitiveness by using design in a targeted manner. While almost half of the companies that do not use design are involved in price wars and are consequently forced to accept falling profit margins, design-oriented companies are part of a decidedly positive trend, with 44 per cent of design companies announcing an increase in turnover. The study lists the economic success factors of design:
– increased turnover, profits and market shares –
greater innovative power – reduced costs – access to new markets – improved corporate image – enhanced communication with customers.

At the Zollverein School, managers become familiar with the views and ways of thinking of a designer, and vice versa. Their eyes are opened to new perspectives and they learn to work together on the development of strategies that will shape the future.

In this way, the Zollverein School conveys the culture of variety on an interdisciplinary level. The Zollverein School uses innovative design skills on business models. Consequently, decisions are not based on past actions, but on future prospects. The Zollverein School considers management to be a design task. Tomorrow's managers learn to understand what makes design so special and how to use it, while tomorrow's designers

learn about the rules of business and economics. Both sides move away from their traditional viewpoints and link their activities to their company's strategy. The Zollverein School will become a place where each culture gets to know the background and the profession of the other.

Moreover, different design cultures will also be given the attention they deserve. Because unlike the globally standardised world of finance, many countries still have their own marked, national design cultures. This relates both to the product language and to the origins of the designers and their work structures.

In short, design offers companies major advantages in terms of time, costs and differentiation. These benefits are there for the taking right now and their potential has certainly not been exhausted. There is also significant potential in the integration of product development, communication and distribution. Despite all these prospects, there are limits to this instrumental way of viewing things because it can quickly be adapted by the competition.

Design can really only release its full power when managers themselves make the empathetic and interpretative skills of designers their own and use these skills to develop strategies. This process-oriented way of viewing things offers a more sustainable competitive edge. Understanding, and not just quantitively measuring, what customers want and need is the key to successful design processes.

Recognising market potentials and anticipating fashions and changes in values is just as important as recognising social, cultural, economic and technological trends at an early stage. According to a study conducted by the British Design Council, 97 per cent of rapidly growing companies get their ideas from their customers in this way. The role of the design-oriented manager as a mediator between the manufacturer and the user has to date been underestimated. Such design-oriented managers are fostered at the Zollverein School.

MANAGEMENT AND DESIGN CAN LEARN FROM ONE ANOTHER

Not least as a result of the increasing global competition on deregulated markets, business is also facing growing challenges. Unfortunately, it is not always equipped with the necessary solutions. Traditional economic theory assumes that every management task can be summed up in a problem that can be clearly defined and for which an optimum solution can be found. However, this theory, which works on stable, growing markets, has long since reached its limitations. Logic and consistent thinking in rules and standards are no longer enough to shape the future.

zollverein summer school

Existing methods of business management must therefore be developed in order to establish new rules of competition, draft new business model, and create new markets. Design is the ideal discipline for this task because it is all about finding solutions for abstract, vague problems. It is therefore hardly surprising that the economic significance of design has increased and will continue to increase in the future.

REDEFINING DESIGN

As design faces ever greater challenges, so the responsibility for taking design-related decisions also grows. Decisions of this kind are becoming increasingly pivotal aspects of corporate strategy. They open up new markets, stimulate product development and influence production processes. Design reveals the potential for rationalisation in existing structures and can be used to optimise processes. Design cannot react to these new challenges if it is reduced to the role of a mere provider of aesthetic design for an environment.

At a time when design is growing in importance, we at the Zollverein School are developing above and beyond design and giving it a new significance.

One key to taking the new challenges facing design into account would appear to lie in a broadened definition of design. Such a definition was introduced into the debate as far back as the 1960s by Herbert A. Simon in his book *Sciences of the Artificial*. Here Simon applies the concept of design to various systems in technology and society: a broader concept of design, which understands today's complex requirements and which operates above and beyond the traditional divide between the natural sciences and the humanities.

This science of the artificial is above all driven by 'reflective practitioners' because they bring with them the awareness of the problems involved and the experience needed to formulate the relevant questions, and not least to introduce new perspectives into design. The Zollverein School will become a place of interchange for such 'reflective practitioners' from various disciplines.

"OUR ABILITY TO DESIGN PROCESSES, PRODUCTS, AND NETWORKS WILL SHAPE OUR POST-INDUSTRIAL CULTURE."   Klaus J. Maack, Member of the Advisory Board of the Zollverein School

Ensuring the process-oriented capabilities of players in business and social systems will be an important task for design in the future. This relates not only to the analysis of such players' adaptability, but also to the shaping of communication processes within individual systems and between different systems.

From an economic point of view, it is no longer the genius or the team that shapes entrepreneurial processes,

but the form of the entire network and the process capabilities of each element within that network. When so many are linked to so much, economic complexity – i.e. the breadth of choice in the decision-making process – inevitably increases, not only in material but also in social terms. It is at this point that new questions regarding the links between management and design arise and it is exactly these questions that will become the subject of research and teaching at the Zollverein School.

When design addresses the shaping of processes, the significance of the design process itself increases. It is not only the result of the design process (e.g. the formal design of products) that must be assessed. In the interests of process optimisation, we must also ask how effective the cooperation between the players in the design process is, how suitable the capabilities of these players are for that process, where it is possible to rationalise the design process, and where resources are purposefully being saved in individual cases in order to optimise the process as a whole.

STRATEGY: REVOLUTIONISING THE EMPIRE OF IDEAS
The Zollverein School considers strategy to be at the heart of corporate development. This is why strategy is the foundation on which its courses, seminars and workshops are built and the common denominator that links them all. Unlike traditional approaches to teaching strategy, the Zollverein School seeks to link content and processes that take into account specific management tasks in change management processes.

The Zollverein School explains how to take into account the imagination of the customers, resources, the company's expertise and cultural, social, and political developments in the field of brand management. A clear definition of how strategic positioning can be expressed in concrete terms and what can be used to secure economic success will be provided. All of this influences business processes, organisational structures and financial planning. "There is huge potential for innovation when designing business processes. This potential can create sustainable strategic competitive advantages." (Prof. Franz Liebl, module director at the Zollverein School).

Examining issues from new perspectives is decisive when it comes to developing independent, coherent strategies. It is not the strict observance of project plans that leads to success, but the repeated evaluation of hypotheses and interim results, re-examining them again and again from all sides and, where necessary, redefining them: How is it? What could it be like? What 'tomorrow' are we designing?

The quintessence of strategy is the continuous application of interpretation or reinterpretation processes

within a company. The initiation and management of interpretation processes (and the transformation processes that frequently follow) is a significant part of the research and tuition programme at the Zollverein School.

HISTORY

At the Emscher Park international construction exhibition in 1999, the white-paper study 'Zollverein 2010' presented the idea of an interdisciplinary, privately-financed, educational and research institution for design within the grounds of the Zeche Zollverein. The institution was given the preliminary name 'Platform Design'. It was meant to be 'an internationally respected pacesetter for design in the 3rd millennium'.

In the Zollverein's project application to the EU for financial support (within the framework of the EU measure of support for structurally weak regions), the close work between teaching and research, on the one hand, and the implementation of these in the working world, on the other hand were emphasized.

Step by step, the institution began to take shape. Aside from the start-up money from the EU, the state North Rhine-Westphalia and the city of Essen, the 'Platform Design' wanted to avoid the need for any more public funds. The 'Platform Design' should be a private college with a public-private partnership supporting it.

After public funds were approved, development continued in content and organization. This can be seen in the name of the institution: design school zollverein d/s/z.

Following the school's founding year, 2002–03, experts from the fields of design, architecture and business have since confirmed the correctness of the path taken with its combination of management and design. They pointed out how unique the school's profile is – and their advice has been to proclaim the 'Zollverein School of Management and Design' loudly and clearly!

THE ORGANIZATIONAL STRUCTURE

The Zollverein School is run by a non-profit public corporation. With its public partners, the University of Duisburg-Essen and the University of Wuppertal and a private partner (Initiativkreis Ruhrgebiet), the Zollverein School has been able to establish a public-private partnership. The business operations of the Zollverein School are divided into three main fields:
– further education – research and development projects – sponsors and donors

In the field of further education we will offer degree courses in co-operation with universities, based upon which students obtain degrees from the cooperating universities. We estimate having between 160 and 180 students in our Masters programmes.

In the field of research and development we are working together with nationally and EU-funded research projects. However, we also want to work closely with businesses and business cooperatives to strive for real business solutions. These are the opportunities when ideas and concepts are created that in turn help secure business start-ups.

The field of sponsors and donors will help us maintain ties to customers and to implement real business practices. Sponsors will be a source for innovative design projects. They can then benefit earlier from project results and they can also turn to the Zollverein for highly-qualified graduates.

The Zollverein will be a lean organization with only a small permanent staff. Courses will be taught by professors from our cooperating universities and lecturers from the world of business. This leanness and flexibility will lead to very low fixed costs.

RESEARCH AND STUDY

Terms such as 'Strategic Design', 'Organisational Design' and 'Design Processes' indicate how far we intend to extend design terms in teaching and research. The Zollverein School offers a programme that provides the instruments for problem *and* project-oriented, decision-making processes, and, as such, actively supports requirements at large.

The Zollverein School offers Masters and Ph.D. degree programmes in the area of 'business design', both full-time and part-time. Acceptance to the Zollverein School is based on a multi-stage admission process in which applicants must prove their technical and professional qualifications; this is in line with the Zollverein's programme directed at further education students.

Design experts have pointed out the necessity of research in the field but very little design research is done in Germany. A major reason for this deficit is the uncertainty surrounding the term design research and how to define the contents of such research.

At the Zollverein School, the main focus is on practical research projects. Research activities will produce new design solutions and based on these solutions, technological innovations can be implemented for accepted products and services.

REGIONAL ACTIVITIES

The privately-funded school will also reach out to the larger public with workshops and lectures. This will include speeches from guest experts from the following fields and professions: management, media design, computer science, film production, philosophy and science. The goal of such events is to increase the public's awareness about design processes and solutions and to make them more transparent. The Zollverein

School will therefore make the contents of such lectures clearly and intelligibly communicable.

The school will be a place where design will be taught, where design can be contemplated and researched, but also a place where design will be used as a possibility for implementing new ideas.

Together with businesses, the Zollverein School will educate students based on practical questions. Companies can put their queries to the Zollverein School or can let their employees actively participate in research and development projects here.

Graduates of the Zollverein School will also be prepared for a world where they are their own bosses. The knowledge they have gained from projects can immediately be used to further their personal development and to market themselves. One important goal of the Zollverein School is that such start-ups are based near the Zeche Zollverein. Offices, agencies and consulting firms will form the foundation of a Design City Zollverein.

READY FOR THE WORLD

Through its situation in the Ruhr district the Zollverein School is closely linked to the Rhine/Ruhr conurbation. With over 5 million inhabitants, this conurbation is a cultural melting pot. Moreover, its high density of international companies provides the ideal backdrop for the Zollverein School's own international orientation. Although only recently established, the Zollverein School is already part of an international network. It fully intends to extend this network and reinforce its position as a European interchange.

Masters and doctorate courses are taught in English. The Zollverein is aiming at reaching agreements with leading national and international educational and research institutions and is also looking for partners in the world of business. Students, teachers and researchers from around the world are welcome to form a 'melting pot' of international excellence on the campus of the Zollverein School.

THE CAMPUS

The Zollverein School is a central element in the restructuring of the World Cultural Heritage Site Zeche Zollverein. The building of the Zollverein School has been designed by the Japanese architects Kazuyo Sejima & Ryue Nishizawa (architectural offices SANAA, Tokyo) and will be a visible symbol of the future of the Zeche Zollverein. It will be a place where design is not only thought about, but also put into action.

The building makes the conceptual foundation of the Zollverein School – one that can be experienced; it is both transparent and filled with secrets and it calls for

kazuyo sejima explains sanaa's design
for the zollverein school

dialogue and cooperation. It holds its own confidently alongside the World Cultural Heritage Site and, at the same time, it is an encouragement for not only the change of the Zollverein location. The interior structure of the building shows the desired flexibility and variability so that it can be altered to suit new requirements.

The campus and the already existent choreographic centre, along with the extension into the surrounding region, allow access to a boulevard of creativity with the building acting as a portal.

The Zollverein School of Management and Design will be a centre for the creative, for researchers and for entrepreneurs with a passion for design from all around the world.

RALPH BRUDER
FIRST PRESIDENT OF THE ZOLLVEREIN SCHOOL
OF MANAGEMENT AND DESIGN

THE CHRONOLOGY OF THE DESIGN AND BUILDING PROCESS

DATE / CHRONOLOGY

COMMENTS

COMPETITION

17.07.2002
COMPETITION PROCESS
The Zollverein development corporation as client draws up an architecture competition for the new *design school zollverein* (d/s/z). Fifteen internationally known architectural practices are invited to take part. In addition to these a further 1,200 practices submit entries by the end of August. Thirty-five of these are chosen to take part in the competition alongside the fifteen practices already referred to.

A decentralised open spatial concept with introverted and extroverted areas seems best suited to the educational concept behind process-oriented design as well as the provision of optimum conditions for the coordination of teaching, research and career development for 150 students. SPATIAL PROGRAMME FOR THE DESIGN SCHOOL ZOLLVEREIN D/S/Z (EXTRACT)

At the first meeting of the founding council of the d/s/z emphasis is laid on the importance of close links between the development of the building and the evolving project concept. RALPH BRUDER, FIRST PRESIDENT OF THE DESIGN SCHOOL ZOLLVEREIN

16.09.2002
INITIAL COLLOQUIUM
In front of representatives of the fifty architectural practices selected, the client and user present the masterplan for the Zollverein world cultural heritage industrial monument as well as the concept behind the *design school zollverein*.

A central aspect of research and teaching at the d/s/z will be the design of processes. Therefore the spatial programme must go far beyond standard studios and workshops. RALPH BRUDER

DATE / CHRONOLOGY   COMMENTS

---

04. / 05.11.2002
JURY 1

Thirty-nine entries are submitted for the first competition phase that is conducted anonymously. In the course of a two-day evaluation process the jury (Hans-Jürgen Best, Prof. Ralph Bruder, Prof. Manfred Hegger, Dr. Ulrich Heinemann, Prof. Klaus Kada, Dr. Wolfgang Roters, Prof. Gerhard Schmitt, Prof. Thomas Sieverts, Prof. Gesine Weinmiller) selects five designs. The respective practises are asked to develop their work further in the second competition phase. The designs chosen are from: SANAA, Tokyo, OMW, Frankfurt, A_lab, Berlin, Maja Lorbeck + Caramel, Vienna, Leeser Architecture, New York

The jury deliberately recommends five very different designs for the second competition phase. The names of the practices concerned are revealed only after the five designs have been chosen. The highly abstract nature of the cube proposed by SANAA responds to the considerable openness of the concept behind the design school zollverein. The self-assured integration of the large volume in the building ensemble of the Zollverein colliery is also seen positively. RALPH BRUDER

11.11.2002 / 16.12.2002
COLLOQUIUM AND INTERMEDIATE COLLOQUIUM

All five practices make use of the opportunity to conduct individual discussions with representatives of d/s/z to work out together a programme of functions and spaces for the building.

What is the atmosphere of the interior like? How flexible or neutral in terms of use is the interior of the d/s/z? What possibilities are seen for a short-term expansion of the existing programme? QUESTIONS TO SANAA

In discussions with SANAA the architects' high level of interest in the concept of the design school zollverein was particularly striking. In searching for answers to the questions put to us by Kazuyo Sejima and Ryue Nishizawa we are repeatedly compelled to make the concept more concrete. In this phase the profile of the design school zollverein is intensively developed further. RALPH BRUDER

RALPH BRUDER THE CHRONOLOGY OF THE DESIGN AND BUILDING PROCESS

DATE / CHRONOLOGY

COMMENTS

27.01.2003
JURY 2 AND CONCLUDING PRESENTATION
The jury unanimously chooses the design presented by SANAA as the competition winner.

This is an example of a rare case where place, commission, the suggested solution and its authors present, in a completely convincing way, a response to a complex competition scenario. PROF. GESINE WEINMILLER, JURY MEMBER

As the future users of the building by SANAA we feel honoured by the jury's choice. The design with its open spatial concept and its well-handled relationship between internal and external space harmonises in an exemplary way with the concept of the design school zollverein. This building, which is sure to attract international attention, responds to the lofty aims of the concept behind the design school. We are certain that in SANAA we have found a most suitable partner for the development of the d/s/z. RALPH BRUDER

PRELIMINARY DESIGN STAGE

11.03.2003
PROJECT MEETING 1
First meeting between the architects and the client, the Zollverein development corporation and the user, *design school zollverein*.

SANAA wishes to make clear that the proposed placing of the building on the site is possible only if the existing production hall of the screw manufacturing company Wilhelmi is demolished. RALPH BRUDER

DATE / CHRONOLOGY	COMMENTS

10.3.2003 – 27.04.2003
EXHIBITION AND LECTURE

In the exhibition 'SANAA – architecture design', conceived especially for the high-pressure compressor hall of the Zollverein colliery 'Shaft XII', Kazuyo Sejima and Ryue Nishizawa also present some of their other current projects alongside their design for the new school building.

We wish to present at as early a stage possible both the plans for the future design school zollverein and the architectural practice SANAA to an interested public. RALPH BRUDER

It is certainly something rather special that someone comes here from Japan to erect a building for us. COMMENT FROM A VISITOR TO THE EXHIBITION

03.04.2003
DISCUSSIONS WITH THE AUTHORITIES AND PROJECT MEETING 2

The first discussions with the Essen municipal authorities are held. At the project meeting 2 SANAA reports that the construction and design of the façade is currently being examined. The client expresses the wish that the light-coloured effect originally planned should be kept, even if the external envelope is to be of exposed concrete.

29.04.2003
PROJECT MEETING 3

SANAA choose the practice of architects Heinrich Böll and Hans Krabel as their German partner office to coordinate with local partners. In addition, the positioning of the building on the site and the schedule are discussed.

If the building is to be placed further back, then, to maintain a balance and taking into account the scale of the surroundings, the building must be of a certain proportion. KAZUYO SEJIMA

RALPH BRUDER THE CHRONOLOGY OF THE DESIGN AND BUILDING PROCESS

DATE / CHRONOLOGY   COMMENTS

30.04.2003
DESIGN MEETING 1
The architects and user discuss the utilization of space within the building. The user expresses the desire that the following aspects should be considered in further planning measures: reduction in size of the reception area on the ground floor to create an exhibition area; office accommodation for 20 teams of five people on the 1st floor; flexible seminar rooms on the 2nd floor.

16. / 17.05.2003
DESIGN MEETING 2
SANAA proposes a new position on the site for their building and – based on the discussions at the first design meeting – presents two models for the use of the internal space. Each level is to have a specific character. The design of the façade is also discussed using models and drawings. The number and size of the openings vary considerably, the current designs show 3,816, 2,466 and 1,288 openings.

At this meeting held in the Tokyo office of SANAA the alterations discussed on the first day are presented on the next in the form of three-dimensional models. From the user's viewpoint reducing the number of window openings but increasing their size is a good proposal. This will alter the impression of a net-like façade with countless openings. RALPH BRUDER

26.05.2003
DESIGN MEETING 3
SANAA presents reworked designs for the internal layout as well as four models of the façade.

The layout of rooms on the 3rd level (the office floor) is much discussed. In the vicinity of the conference room a place for informal meetings is needed. The glass walls on the 3rd level mean that SANAA's concept of open spatial structures can be harmonised with the user's wish for areas that can be partitioned off. RALPH BRUDER

DATE / CHRONOLOGY	COMMENTS

27.5.2003
PROJECT MEETING 4
The position of the *design school zollverein* on the site of the Zollverein world cultural heritage site is finally determined.

25.06.2003
DESIGN MEETING 4 AND PROJECT MEETING 5
To examine the incidence of daylight in the building, SANAA undertakes studies in Tokyo and produces full-scale models of the façade openings. On this basis they present three proposals for the design of the office level. By the next meeting the incidence of light on the various levels is to be examined in greater detail – possibly larger façade openings will be required. In addition a new schedule will be drawn up. Delays in the Wilhelmi Company's vacation of the premises will delay the demolition of the old buildings and, as a consequence, the start of construction of the *design school zollverein*.

Although the new, large windows significantly increase the quality of the building in use, for us as users as well as for the client time is needed to get used to fewer but larger windows. However the reduction of the building costs resulting from this measure is a very powerful argument indeed. RALPH BRUDER

16.07.2003
PRESENTATION OF THE PRELIMINARY PLANNING
SANAA and Böll present the preliminary planning. The commissioned engineering offices also introduce their work: the structure of the external façades (SAPS and Bollinger + Grohmann), building services engineering (Transplan) and the energy concept (Transsolar).

Both user and client are very satisfied with the focussed development of the design. The vision of receiving a building that responds to the new concept for the design school zollverein becomes increasingly concrete. RALPH BRUDER

RALPH BRUDER THE CHRONOLOGY OF THE DESIGN AND BUILDING PROCESS

DATE / CHRONOLOGY	COMMENTS
DETAILED DESIGN STAGE	
28.07.2003 COORDINATING DISCUSSION The partners involved in the planning process discuss all the points that require special attention at the detailed design stage. These include the light situation and the internal organisation of the 3rd floor, as well as the use of the ground floor. The projected 'think tanks' (cubicles) or their installation at a later date are incorporated in the plan.	On the first floor, that has a ceiling height of c. 10 metres, two boxes with a floor area of 10 x 5 metres each are to be suspended from the ceiling. These 'cubicles' are to be used by research teams who need space to work intensively on a particular problem. RALPH BRUDER
21.08.2003 DESIGN MEETING 5 The discussion about the design of the façade and the use of the internal space is continued.	Dear Prof. Bruder, [...] As we already discussed during the design meeting [...], attached you will receive the floor plan as a basis for your consideration of office allocation in accordance with the given layout. Please note that some rooms allow for two types of functions. E-MAIL NICOLE BERGANSKI, SANAA, 30.09.2005

DATE / CHRONOLOGY	COMMENTS

12.09.2003
DISCUSSION TO AGREE ON POTENTIAL TO CUT COSTS
Client and user discuss what elements could be dispensed with, should it prove necessary to reduce costs. The items discussed include the overall reduction of size (rejected), dropping the second lift (rejected), doing without the top cover (rejected), eliminating the 'think tanks' on the first floor (accepted).

Despite the restricted budget, together with the other project partners we are looking for solutions that still allow us to develop a high-quality building that is suited to the needs of the users. The discussions this involves are at times most intensive but always very constructive. RALPH BRUDER

21.10.2003
PRESENTATION OF THE CONCEPT OF ACTIVE THERMAL INSULATION
The Transsolar company, which has been involved in the development of the building since the competition phase, presents the energy concept. The idea is to insulate and heat the building with the help of water already available in the mineshafts that is pumped from a depth of 1,000 metres into the Zollverein at a temperature of 30 degrees Celsius. This 'active' thermal insulation can halve the amount of heating energy required by the building. Additionally, it allows the external walls to be made far thinner than originally planned which would facilitate the concept behind the design. In the next step agreement on this matter must be reached with Deutsche Steinkohle AG.

The concept of active thermal insulation is an innovation in the area of building insulation that was not initially planned for this project. This is the first time that this concept will be used in Europe. RALPH BRUDER

RALPH BRUDER THE CHRONOLOGY OF THE DESIGN AND BUILDING PROCESS

DATE / CHRONOLOGY

COMMENTS

01.12.2003
MEETING OF THE PARTNERS OF THE DESIGN SCHOOL ZOLLVEREIN
The meeting of the partners decides to change the name of the *design school zollverein* to *Zollverein School of Management and Design*. The former founding president of the d/s/z Prof. Ralph Bruder is appointed president of the Zollverein School of Management and Design.

The new name refers to the place where the institution was founded as well as making clear the Zollverein School aims at establishing a link between creative, innovative ideas and their application in the business world. RALPH BRUDER

18.11.2003
PROJECT MEETING 8
Deutsche Steinkohle AG agrees in principal to water being pumped from the mine to provide the thermal insulation of the façade. In the next step the technical requirements are to be specified. There are further delays in the Wilhelmi Company's vacation of the site – the buildings cannot therefore be demolished until the end of 2004.

19.12.2003
PRESENTATION OF THE DETAILED DESIGN
The general planner SANAA/Böll presents the design to representatives of the State of Nordrhein-Westfalen, the City of Essen, Deutsche Steinkohle AG, the NRW regional development association, as well as the client and the user. The building is to have more than 120 openings in four different sizes.

We conclude 2003 with the confident feeling that we will obtain a good building that not only responds excellently to our requirements but also contains many technical innovations. RALPH BRUDER

DATE / CHRONOLOGY	COMMENTS

IMPLEMENTATION DESIGN STAGE

09.02.2004
4TH DISCUSSION

The project partners discuss the details that have resulted from the detailed design planning that must be worked out at the implementation stage. The Zollverein School is asked to indicate to what extend the ground floor area can be used publicly.	The public use of the ground floor is of major importance to the Zollverein School. On the ground floor exhibitions will be held, there will be a cafeteria open to the general public, and public lectures and presentations will take place in the lecture hall. The Zollverein School wants to encourage the public to visit the building. RALPH BRUDER

01. / 02.03.2004
DISCUSSION ON STATUS OF DETAILED DESIGN

User, client and general planner discuss planning details, in particular the floor finishes on the different levels (rubber flooring is proposed), as well as the acoustics of the auditorium, the seminar rooms on the 2nd floor and the offices on the 3rd floor level.	As the details of the interior concept are gradually finalised the understanding of how the Zollverein School will operate becomes clearer. This includes in particular the question at what times which people will be on what floors and in which rooms and how these people will move from floor to floor. RALPH BRUDER

02.04.2004
PRESS CONFERENCE

SANAA, Transsolar, d/s/z and the Zollverein development corporation present the final design and the energy concept for the building to the public.	The architectural design is completed and the concept of the Zollverein School has also crystallised. The first study course is being developed and the future lecturers have met on several occasions. RALPH BRUDER

RALPH BRUDER THE CHRONOLOGY OF THE DESIGN AND BUILDING PROCESS

DATE / CHRONOLOGY   COMMENTS

20.07.2004
PRESENTATION OF THE CONCEPTS FOR THE FAÇADE
CONSTRUCTION

SANAA/Böll present concepts for heat retention in relation to various external wall constructions and show the effects on the running costs of the building. It must be clarified how the building can be insulated if Deutsche Steinkohle AG stops or interrupts the supply of water extracted from the mine.

The external walls have a large number of window openings of different sizes, the intention being that they should not form any legible geometrical pattern for viewers outside the building. Equally, the load-bearing structure as well as the lines of the floors should not be expressed in the external envelope. The external walls should be as thin as possible. EXTRACT FROM THE CONCEPT FOR THE FAÇADE CONSTRUCTION BY SANAA/BÖLL

27.07.2004
PLANNING DISCUSSION

It is agreed that if the supply of water from the mine is stopped the building must be equipped with externally or internally mounted thermal insulation.

As mining experts from DMT and DSK were not in a position to provide any definite statements or a political decision about the supply of water from the mine, and although it is not expected in the foreseeable future that the supply will be stopped, we propose a fall-back solution for the client so that internal thermal insulation could be fitted later, if required. E-MAIL ANDREAS KRAWCZYK, BÜRO BÖLL/KRABEL, 27.07.2004

6.12.2004
TENDER FOR THE PRIMARY STRUCTURE

JANUARY 2005
PRESENTATION DURING THE IMM COLOGNE 2005

The Zollverein School presents its innovative curriculum during imm Cologne 2005 in the *Stylepark*.

The spaces designed by SANAA for the Stylepark presentation attract additional attention. RALPH BRUDER

DATE / CHRONOLOGY	COMMENTS

26.01.2005
DISCUSSIONS IN TOKYO

At a discussion between the architects and Ralph Bruder various possibilities for reducing costs are examined. These include, for example, the flooring – carpet is now proposed instead of rubber. In the seminar rooms on the 2nd floor instead of glass walls opaque partitions will be used. Glazed cut outs will be added in these partitions. The sliding glass wall in the conference room is also dropped.

24.2.2005
COMMENCEMENT OF STUDIES

The eighteen students of the first year commence their studies at the Zollverein School. Lectures are provisionally held on the world cultural heritage site in a former coal grading hall.

Our first students form a creative and highly motivated team. We are looking forward to spending two interesting years together. RALPH BRUDER

MARCH 2005
E-MAIL SANAA / ZOLLVEREIN

Work on fitting-out the interiors is becoming more concrete. The plans of the various floors and the furnishings and fittings are adapted on the basis of the alterations discussed in Tokyo in January. The precise positioning of the cafeteria counter and the reception desk on the ground floor are determined. The change of materials for the partition walls on the 2nd floor has made it necessary to alter the layout of the seminar rooms. It has now been decided to dispense with the small seminar room at 2nd floor level.

Minor alterations have had to be made to the layout of the 2nd floor due to the elimination of the small seminar room and the use of plasterboard walls for the other rooms. As the opaque walls meant that the lighting and spatial situation was no longer satisfactory, the large seminar rooms have been shifted in the direction of the staircase core. This produces a more compact circulation system and a more generously dimensioned space at the rear wall of the large seminar rooms. E-MAIL ANDREAS KRAWCZYK, SANAA

RALPH BRUDER THE CHRONOLOGY OF THE DESIGN AND BUILDING PROCESS

DATE / CHRONOLOGY

COMMENTS

CONSTRUCTION PHASE

17.03.2005
GROUND-BREAKING CEREMONY
The start of construction of the Zollverein School is celebrated with a press conference and a ceremony attended by Michael Vesper, the Minister for Urban Development, Housing, Culture and Sport in the State of NRW. A meeting is held with Nicole Berganski on the design of the reception and the cafeteria counter.

The first students of the Zollverein School attended this celebration. The goal of developing the concept of the Zollverein School parallel to the construction process has been achieved. The first student generation will be able to present their degree work in the newly opened building. RALPH BRUDER

APRIL 2005
E-MAIL SANAA / ZOLLVEREIN
On the basis of earlier discussions SANAA has adapted the internal layout once again. The position of the conference room has been changed: the lounge counter on the 2nd floor has been shifted from the lift core to the nearby staircase core.

We are particularly happy with the new layout of the 3rd floor. Some further minor questions (e.g. as regards further doors) have arisen. E-MAIL RALPH BRUDER, 01.04.2005

For reasons of expense we have attempted to reduce the number of doors as far as possible. E-MAIL NICOLE BERGANSKI, 04.04.2005

END OF SEPTEMBER 2005
MEETING ABOUT THE PRESENT STAGE OF PLANNING OF FURNITURE AND FITTINGS
SANAA suggests changing the material for the lounge counters. Instead of concrete it is now planned to make them of expanded metal.

DATE / CHRONOLOGY	COMMENTS

13.10.2005
BUILDING SITE CELEBRATION OF THE ZOLLVEREIN SCHOOL
Prof. Ralph Bruder, founding president of the Zollverein School and Roland Weiss, managing director of the Zollverein development company are handed the foundation stone for the new school building by the architect Ryue Nishizawa.

The foundation stone contents a contribution by the two architects who make up SANAA, Kazuyo Sejima and Ryue Nishizawa, a newspaper of the current day as well as contributions from first year students and a current set of euro coins. PRESS REPORT OF THE ZOLLVEREIN SCHOOL (EXTRACT)

12.11.2005
MEETING IN TOKYO
Ralph Bruder and Roland Weiss, the managing director of the Zollverein development corporation meet with the architects in Tokyo to discuss the final planning details. Models of the furniture are presented. The Zollverein School will look for a partner to choose the furnishings jointly with SANAA.

16.01.2006
LANDSCAPE DESIGN
SANAA make a proposal for the design of the outdoor areas.

15 FEBRUARY 2006
TOPPING OUT CEREMONY OF THE ZOLLVEREIN SCHOOL
With representatives of the general planner, the client, the user, the state government, the city of Essen, the developer. All neighbours, friends and supporters are invited to view the building,

In the meantime a second year of students have started their studies at the Zollverein School of Management and Design. They all look forward to moving into their new building in June 2006. RALPH BRUDER

KAZUYO SEJIMA + RYUE NISHIZAWA / SANAA

THE ZOLLVEREIN SCHOOL OF MANAGEMENT AND DESIGN
2003 – 2006

The project developed through close collaboration and the joint definition of spatial needs by both the user and the client.

The building – that measures 35×35 metres and is 34 metres high – relates to the scale of the Zollverein colliery. At the same time, by recessing the new building, it responds to the neighbouring buildings in the street space.

The idea of stacking open floor plans developed as a consequence of responding to requirements and to the different character of the various functions. Each level has been developed through close examination, and the functional characteristics of the second and third levels in particular have been worked out very specifically.

The first level – the design studio – is the production level and contains the creative workplaces that are augmented by the calm and subdued work atmosphere on the level above. This latter level contains the library and the freely positioned seminar rooms, as well as a number of quiet individual workplaces along the north façade.

Above this is the office level with work areas of different size and character that are separated by glass partition walls. Window openings in the external walls as well as courtyards distributed in plan guarantee daylight and visual connections for all work areas.

The façades contain the volume, but, through the apparently random arrangement of differently sized openings across the entire façade, the surroundings and the interior engage in a highly unusual interactive relationship. The position of the openings is determined both by the function of the space inside as well as by the orientation.

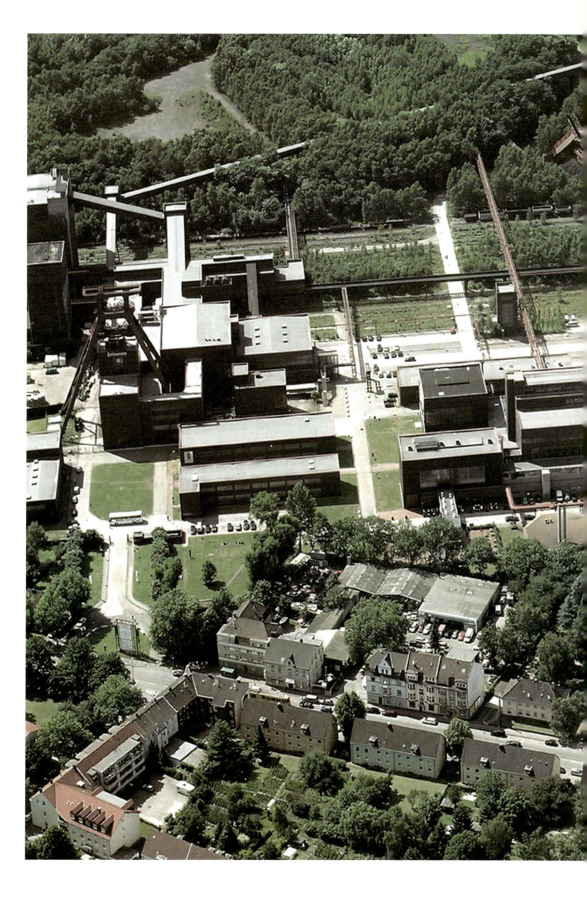

KAZUYO SEJIMA + RYUE NISHIZAWA / SANAA
THE ZOLLVEREIN SCHOOL OF MANAGEMENT AND DESIGN 2003–2006

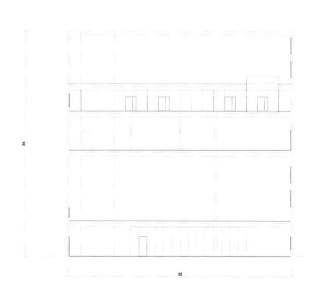

section

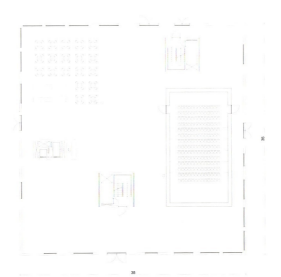

ground floor

first level

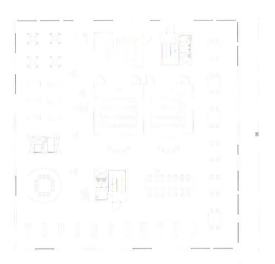

second level

third level

roof garden

107

MATTHIAS SCHULER, TRANSSOLAR
ENERGY CONCEPT

NICOLE BERGANSKI, SANAA
DESIGN CONCEPT

COLLABORATION BETWEEN ENERGY AND DESIGN

SITE CONDITIONS

As a precursor to any integrated energy concept site research is vital, paying particular attention to such conditions as macroclimate, microclimate, noise levels, air quality, soil conditions and available energy sources. Essen has a very moderate climate, seldom reaching temperatures below freezing or above 30°C.

15 years ago the former coalmine Zeche Zollverein ceased active digging, but the mineshafts and tunnels have remained open to a depth of 1000 m, allowing for possible future use.

Consequently the DSK – Deutsche Steinkohle AG – the public owner of the mines, has been continually pumping water from this depth to avoid flooding. This water, partially contaminated with heavy metals and minerals, with an average temperature of 29°C, is fed into the river Emsch at a rate of 600 m³/h. This is a remarkable energy source crying out for use.

OVERALL CONCEPT

The Zollverein School is located between an old industrial site and a suburban area. The new building volume is designed to act as an entrance and marker for the whole area, its size being an important element. The cube relates to the scale of the former coalmine Zeche Zollverein, acting as an attractor for the site. At the same time it responds to the neighbouring houses, setback from the street.

The scheme is intended to charge the area between the Zollverein School and the former coalmine buildings with differences in ambience. The building is big, new and prominently placed, while at the same time relating to different areas within the Zollverein site.

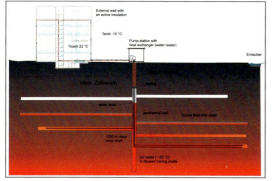

conceptual diagram showing the existing position of the pumps and the connection for utilizing the water in the mine shaft to supply warm water to the design school

MATTHIAS SCHULER, TRANSSOLAR
ENERGY CONCEPT

NICOLE BERGANSKI, SANAA
DESIGN CONCEPT

ENERGY CONCEPT

Given this free, renewable energy potential we proposed a heat exchanger at the top of the mining shaft, using part of the water flow to heat up a secondary water circuit, which then delivers heat to the Zollverein School. The secondary circuit is required because of the mine water's low quality. Water analysis and material testing prior to ground breaking has proven the system's feasibility. Permission to use the water for as long as it is being pumped has been granted to the building owner by the DSK. Although no one knows when the DSK will close the mine and shut off the water flow, different scenarios have been evaluated, such as installing a heat exchanger in the mining tunnels or the Zollverein School itself pumping off the mine water, which will be limited to a depth of 200–300 m, the expected water level after pumping has stopped.

The heat exchanger station is positioned close to the former shafts 1/2/8 and connected via underground piping to the Zollverein School, protecting historical views of the site.

To use this natural heat source from the mine water requires a heating system which can operate at temperatures of 27–30°C. A radiant heating system within the exposed concrete ceilings was therefore chosen. The system can be reversed in summer for

BUILDING CONCEPT

The Zollverein School deliberately fronts all directions in both form and use. It is a large abstract volume – a landmark with a strong presence.

Public functions are concentrated on the ground level. One entrance is situated on Gelsenkirchener Strasse, another faces the Zollverein site. The first upper level, the design studio, has the highest clearance for a maximum flexibility and a pleasant atmosphere fostering a creative working environment. The second upper level contains the library. The seminar rooms are spread out and boast different characteristics, with a number of quiet work places being provided along the northeast façade. On the third upper level, offices are arranged around courtyards allowing for daylight, natural ventilation and views from each workstation. The uppermost level is conceived as a partly covered roof garden.

The section of the Zollverein School is a study of different heights for different functions. All levels have high ceilings but each floor is different. The building consists of stacked open floor plans ranging from vast indoor spaces to a covered outdoor space. These characteristics combined with large spans and free circulation contribute to a high degree of flexibility and diversity on each level; resulting in a variety of changing paths, meeting points and

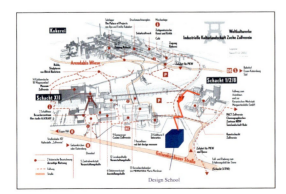

site plan of the zeche zollverein showing the planned location and the remote heating conduits for the utilization of mine shaft water

MATTHIAS SCHULER, TRANSSOLAR
ENERGY CONCEPT

NICOLE BERGANSKI, SANAA
DESIGN CONCEPT

night-time activation of the thermal mass via an evaporative cooling tower.

Conversely, the water can be used to preheat the intake air.

The total, maximum heating demand of the building – including the active insulation system, described in the next section, is 540 kW, which can be met by the mining water at a temperature of 29/25°C.

interaction, reflecting the dynamic spirit of the Zollverein School.

The large space on the first upper level can be used to integrate temporary cubicles. On top of the building there is a flexible in-between area, the roof garden. It offers the possibility for temporary extension, but could equally well be used as an exhibition space.

BUILDING ENVELOPE

The competition phase façade, evaluated in an early design stage, did not meet the daylight levels required by regulations due to the combination of small openings and a 0.5 m thick façade. In an intensive step-by-step exchange with the architects, we evaluated and visualized different solutions with more openings, larger openings, or the use of inward sloping windowsills. The final design and distribution of the fenestration was based on the different functional requirements on the different levels, each one demanding different daylight conditions.

FAÇADE CONCEPT

The main concept of the façade is its role as a filter for the surrounding landscape. The external walls enclose the volume, yet through the apparent randomness of the arrangement of square holes, the exterior and interior spaces initiate a subtle interaction. The position of each opening has been decided in accordance with the function of the space within and its orientation towards the sun. The openings allow for views of the surrounding area and offer natural illumination. In combination with the particular ceiling heights of the floors, this renders the interior a bright and comfortable daylight space.

photograph of model of exterior

MATTHIAS SCHULER, TRANSSOLAR
ENERGY CONCEPT

NICOLE BERGANSKI, SANAA
DESIGN CONCEPT

The thick wall construction, determined by the heat conservation regulations and the design's request for a visually coherent concrete wall, without any expansion joints, arrived at a thickness of more than 0.5 m. This not only reduced the daylight intake, but also made the smaller windows look more like holes. A reduction of the insulation level in the double shell concrete wall by a few centimetres could not solve the problem.

The rethinking of the free energy source on the Zollverein School location, namely the mine water, initiated a completely new approach towards 'active insulation'.

This system uses a 0.3 m-thick monolithic, concrete wall, which contains plastic pipes that heat the wall with the energy harnessed from the mine water. The 'active' insulation must ensure a temperature above 18°C on the inner surface of the wall. Long and very engaged discussions within the design team finally led to this system, with the understanding that approximately 80% of the wall heat would be lost to the outside environment through the non-insulated, external wall surface, but our free and CO_2-free energy source allowed for such losses.

Together with the engineers, appropriate illumination levels were designed after the competition phase by positioning the openings in accordance with the structural system and a calculated daylight simulation. The competition scheme, with its many small openings, was revised in an effort to create pleasant, well-lit spaces. The sizes of the openings were developed in order to achieve moderate levels of illumination throughout the building, but the lighting situation on every floor differs in accordance with each function.

The translation of the basic façade concept into the final design was successful, and we feel confident that the resulting composition is a well-balanced arrangement. A clear structure, light surfaces and the façade openings generate a feeling of spaciousness within the building. A creative workspace on the first upper level has been created with homogenous lighting and material.

The walls are of exposed, light-coloured concrete, both inside and out, but the material itself can be seen beyond its surface attributes and the walls made as thin as possible. The implementation of active insulation using the mine water allowed for a single concrete layer, which offers a slim and unblemished outer wall.

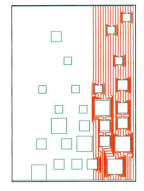

pipes set in concrete wall showing optimal course of piping in external wall

MATTHIAS SCHULER, TRANSSOLAR
ENERGY CONCEPT

NICOLE BERGANSKI, SANAA
DESIGN CONCEPT

A detailed analysis by the design team of both the consistent and transient behaviour of the wall temperature during the whole year dictated a distance of 0.4 m between pipes. Intensive discussion with the structural engineers ensured that the piping system could be integrated with the reinforcement in the wall. By tempering the wall through the active insulation system, the crack dimensions could be limited to imperceptible levels, without increased reinforcement. If necessary the pipes could become denser around the windows to avoid T-pieces and different pipe sizes.

Even with the integrated piping system the monolithic concrete wall was remarkably cheaper than the double shell concrete wall, saving more money than had been spent on the mine water system.

To prevent freezing of the wall piping system during a system pump failure, a self emptying concept was developed, which is activated at a critical temperature in the wall. Energy flow and control parameters were determined using dynamic building and system simulations with the simulation package TRNSYS. Aware of the short construction phase of the project, the design team developed a strategy for the installation of the wall piping system, one that even influenced the final design of the reinforcement in the wall.

The construction is simple due to the façades' role as the primary structure. The supporting external walls and the cavity ceilings allow for wide spans through the interior spaces. The floor areas are flexible, being unhindered by structural requirements.

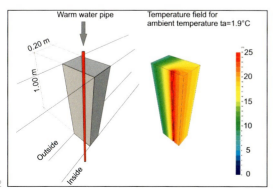

distribution of temperature in a wall around a pipe

MATTHIAS SCHULER, TRANSSOLAR
ENERGY CONCEPT

NICOLE BERGANSKI, SANAA
DESIGN CONCEPT

CONCLUSION

The energy supply concept for the Zollverein School is based on mine water, the CO_2-free heat source. This is a very strong local reference for the project, allowing a 'unique' and outstanding energy concept. This is only possible in the case of the Zollverein School in Essen, not for any design school in any place.

The direct energy distribution concept with slab heating and active insulation allows the use of the mining water natural heat source without a heat pump to increase the temperature. The active insulation allows a simpler and cheaper monolithic wall construction, reinforcing the architectural concept of the building envelope. The concept reaches a heating energy consumption which is 75% below regulation and which saves heating operation cost – 7,000 €/a and reduces the CO_2 load of the building by 31 tons/a. This concept has already spurned thoughts for further local mine water use.

CONCLUSION

The Zollverein School will make a remarkable impression with its façade and volume. It relates to the large industrial buildings around it while appearing almost scaleless in its own right.

The stacked floors have different exceptionally high ceilings that relate to the functions they contain and their respective environment.

Generous space is wrapped in a thin outer layer pierced with large openings that force interaction between the interior and the site.

Situated in extraordinary surroundings, the Zollverein School is a unique project that offers the opportunity of developing a specific building envelope which relates to the programme. The design of the façade responds to the function on each level. The result is an exceptional building.

THE BUILDING SITE

THE BUILDING SITE

THE BUILDING SITE

THE BUILDING SITE

KAZUYO SEJIMA + RYUE NISHIZAWA / SANAA

KAZUYO SEJIMA

1956   Born in Ibaraki Prefecture
Graduated from Japan Women's University
with Masters Degree in Architecture
Joined Toyo Ito & Associates
1987   Established Kazuyo Sejima & Associates
1995   Established SANAA with Ryue Nishizawa
2001– Professor at Keio University

RYUE NISHIZAWA

1966   Born in Kanagawa Prefecture
Graduated from Yokohama National University
with Masters Degree in Architecture
Joined Kazuyo Sejima & Associates
1995   Established SANAA with Kazuyo Sejima
1997   Established Office of Ryue Nishizawa
2001– Associate Professor at Yokohama
National University

MAJOR WORKS

1996   Multimedia Workshop, Gifu, Japan
S-House, Okayama, Japan
1997   N-Museum, Wakayama, Japan
M-House, Tokyo, Japan
K-Building, Ibaraki, Japan
1998   Koga Park Café, Ibaraki, Japan
1999   O-Museum, Nagano, Japan
2000   Day Care Center, Kanagawa, Japan
Venice Biennale, 7th International Architecture Exhibition
'City of Girls' Japanese Pavilion, Venice, Italy
PRADA Beauty Prototype
2001   PRADA Beauty LEEGARDEN Hong Kong,
Hong Kong, China
Garden Cafe at the 7th International Istanbul Biennal,
Istanbul, Turkey
2003   ISSEY MIYAKE by NAOKI TAKIZAWA,
Tokyo, Japan
Christian Dior Building Omotesando, Tokyo, Japan
2004   21st-Century Museum of Contemporary Art
Kanazawa, Kanazawa Japan

CURRENT PROJECTS

Stadstheater Almere 'De Kunstlinie', Almere,
The Netherlands
The Toledo Museum of Art Glass Pavilion, Toledo,
Ohio, USA

Extension to the Institut Valencia d'Art Modern,
Valencia, Spain
Zollverein School of Management and Design,
Essen, Germany
New Museum of Contemporary Art, New York, USA
House for China International Practical Exhibition
of Architecture, Nanjing, China
Novartis Campus WSJ-158 Office Building, Basle,
Switzerland
Naoshima Ferrey Terminal, Kagawa, Japan
Learning Centre, EPFL (École Polytechnique
Fédérale de Lausanne), Switzerland
Louvre Lens, Paris, France

AWARDS

1998 The Prize of Architectural Institute of Japan, Tokyo
2000 Erich Schelling Architekturpreis, Kalsruhe, Germany
2002 Arnold W. Brunner Memorial Prize in Architecture,
American Academy of Arts & Letters, N.Y, USA
Architecture Award of Salzburg Vincenzo Scamozzi,
Salzburg, Austria
2004 Golden Lion for the most remarkable work in the
exhibition Metamorph in the 9th International Architecture
Exhibition, Venice Biennale, Italy
46th Mainichi Newspaper Arts Award
(Architecture Category)
The Rolf Schock Prize in category of visual arts, Sweden

SELECTED PUBLICATIONS

Special issue, Kazuyo Sejima & Associates 1987–1996,
Kenchiku Bunka, vol. 51 No.591, Shokokusha Publishing
Co. Ltd, Japan
Monograph, Kazuyo Sejima 1988–1996, EL CROQUIS,
No.77 (I), Spain
Special issue, Kazuyo Sejima 1987–1999 /
Kazuyo Sejima + Ryue Nishizawa 1995–1999, JA vol. 35,
SHINKENCHIKU-SHA Co. Ltd, Japan
2000 Monograph, Kazuyo Sejima + Ryue Nishizawa
1995–2000, EL CROQUIS, No.99, Spain
2003 Monograph, KAZUYO SEJIMA + RYUE NISHIZAWA
/ SANAA WORKS 1995–2003 TOTO Shuppan, Japan
Kazuyo Sejima + Ryue Nishizawa 2000/2004,
EL CROQUIS, No.121/122, Spain
2005 GA Sejima Kazuyo + Nishizawa Ryue Dokuhon,
A.D.A, EDITA, Japan

BUILDING DATA

COMPETITION
Building footprint: 1,432 m² (37.85 × 37.85 m)
Height: 35.75 m
Main usable floor area: 4,368 m² (1,243 m² roof)
Gross floor area: 5,854 m² (1,309 m² roof)
Gross building volume: 51,216 m³

ARCHITECTS
Kazuyo Sejima + Ryue Nishizawa / SANAA, Tokyo
LANDSCAPE ARCHITECTURE
Kazuyo Sejima + Ryue Nishizawa / SANAA, Tokyo
STRUCTURAL ENGINEERS
SAPS / Sasaki and Partners, Tokyo

PLANNING
Building footprint: 1,225 m² (35 × 35 m)
Height: 34 m
Main usable floor area / above ground: 3,770 m²
incl. roof gardens (968 m² roof)
Net floor area / above ground: 4,830 m²
incl. roof gardens (1,037 m² roof)
Gross floor area / above ground: 4,900 m²
(410 m² split-level / 1,067 m² roof)
Net floor area / lower level: 1,108 m²
Gross floor area/ lower level: 1,225 m²
Gross building volume / above ground: 41,650 m³
Gross volume / lower level: 5,145 m³

ARCHITECTS
Kazuyo Sejima + Ryue Nishizawa / SANAA, Tokyo
GENERAL PLANNER
Kazuyo Sejima + Ryue Nishizawa / SANAA, Tokyo
Architekturbüro Heinrich Böll
STRUCTURAL ENGINEERS
SAPS / Sasaki and Partners, Tokio
B+G Ingenieure / Bollinger und Grohmann GmbH
BUILDING SERVICES ENGINEERS
Transplan Technik-Bauplanung GmbH
with Winter Ingenieure
AIR CONDITIONING + ENERGY / LIGHTING
Transsolar Energietechnik GmbH
BUILDING PHYSICS
Horstmann + Berger
BUILDING AND ROOM ACOUSTICS
Müller-BBM GmbH
FIRE PROTECTION
Hagen Ingenieure für Brandschutz

THE AUTHORS

NICOLE KERSTIN BERGANSKI graduated from the Technical University, Berlin, in 1999. From 1999 – 2001 she worked at sauerbruch hutton architects and, since 2002, has been project architect at SANAA, Tokyo, responsible for the Zollverein School in Essen and the WSJ-158 Office Building on the Novartis Campus in Basle. She has recently opened her own office in Frankfurt/Main, Germany.

From 1996 – 2005 RALPH BRUDER was professor for Ergonomics in Design at the University of Duisburg-Essen and head of the Institute for Ergonomics and Design Research, which he founded. From 1998 – 2002 Bruder was dean of the department of Design and Art at the University of Essen. In April 2002, he was appointed first president of the design school zollverein (now the Zollverein School of Management and Design) and, in 2006, professor for Ergonomics and head of the Institute for Ergonomics at the TU Darmstadt.

The art historian KRISTIN FEIREISS is head of the architecture forum AedesBerlin. She is also one of the founding members of the Zollverein School of Management and Design, established in 2002. Feireiss now works as a publicist, presenter and freelance curator of architecture exhibitions in Germany and abroad. She is the editor of a number of monographs and publications in the field of architecture and urban culture, and is publishing and text editor at AedesBerlin Verlag.

The mechanical engineer MATTHIAS SCHULER founded the climate engineering consulting company TRANSSOLAR in 1992 which integrates energy-saving and comfort-orientated measures into the building design stage. He has worked on national and international projects with Frank O. Gehry, Ben van Berkel and Helmut Jahn, among others. Schuler is also visiting professor at the GSD at Harvard University.

Academic positions held by the architect and town planner THOMAS SIEVERTS include professor for planning and urban design from 1967 – 1971 in Berlin, visiting professor at Harvard University in the early 1970s and professor at the TU Darmstadt from 1971 – 1999. From 1978 – 2005 Sieverts ran his own planning office in Bonn. He also has extensive international experience as a competition judge, consultant and lecturer.

The architect DEYAN SUDJIC is the architecture critic of the Observer and editor of Domus. He is also visiting professor at the Royal College of Art and, between 1992 and 1996, for design theory at the Hochschule für Angewandte Kunst in Vienna. He directed the architecture biennale in Venice in 2002 and has curated numerous other exhibitions on architecture and design. In 1983 he founded Blueprint and remained its editor for 12 years, later working as the director of Glasgow 1999: *UK City of Architecture and Design*.

© Prestel Verlag,
Munich · Berlin · London · New York 2006

© for the illustrations by SANAA, with the exception of
the following: pp. 14/15: Peter Wieler/Essen Marketing,
pp. 92/93: Peter Wieler/Essen Marketing and SANAA,
pp. 18–21: OMA office, pp. 22–25, 41, 59, 61, 69–75,
114–123: Thomas Mayer Archive/Zollverein School, p. 56:
Site photographs: Christopher Dawson/Visualization by
SANAA, pp. 108, 109, 111, 112: Transsolar: Christian Matt,
Matthias Schuler

Prestel Verlag
Königinstrasse 9, 80539 Munich
Tel. +49 (89) 38 17 09-0; Fax +49 (89) 38 17 09-35
www.prestel.de

Prestel Publishing Ltd.
4, Bloomsbury Place, London WC1A 2QA
Tel. +44 (20) 7323-5004; Fax +44 (20) 7636-8004

Prestel Publishing
900 Broadway, Suite 603, New York, NY 10003
Tel. +1 (212) 995-2720; Fax +1 (212) 995-2733
www.prestel.com

Prestel books are available worldwide. Please contact
your nearest bookseller or one of the above addresses
for information concerning your local distributor.

Library of Congress Control Number: 2006904287

British Library Cataloguing-in-Publication Data: a
catalogue record for this book is available from the
British Library; Deutsche Nationalbibliothek holds a record
of this publication in the Deutsche Nationalbibliografie;
detailed bibliographical data can be found under:
http://dnb.ddb.de

Concept: Kristin Feireiss and Angeli Sachs
in cooperation with Nicole Berganski
Editorial direction: Victoria Salley, Anja Besserer
Translations: James Roderick O'Donovan
Copy-edited by: Christopher Wynne
Design and layout: WIGEL, Munich
Origination: Reproline Genceller, Munich
Printing: sellier druck GmbH, Freising
Binding: Conzella, Pfarrkirchen

Printed in Germany on acid-free paper.

ISBN 3-7913-3539-1
ISBN 978-3-7913-3539-1

Grants from

European Union – European
Regional Development Fund

State of North Rhine-Westphalia

City of Essen